Ed Wells
Partnership

A Joint SPEEA/Boeing Initiative

Providing training and career
development resources for
SPEEA-represented employees
to enhance their technical and
professional skills

10-18 building, MC 6X1-01
635 Park Ave North
Renton, WA   98057-5583

....

http://edwells.web.boeing.com
Phone 425-965-4310

PRAISE FOR
WOMAN OF INFLUENCE

Linear or conventional pathways to leadership really do not exist. Jo's book helps all of us begin where we are, with a thought-provoking and practical process that helps identify our leadership strengths, develop a leader's mindset, and ultimately own the trajectory of our career.

—**Carmen Twillie Ambar**, president of Oberlin College

Jo Miller gets it exactly right. You establish yourself as a leader by being clear about what you authentically have to offer and then translating your strengths in a way that compels notice. This self-marketing matters as much as all the hard work and heavy lifting you do, which is why Jo's book is essential for women seeking to navigate a satisfying path forward.

—**Sally Helgesen**, author of *How Women Rise, The Female Advantage*, and *The Web of Inclusion*

Your performance does not speak for itself. That is what I tell women leaders when they negotiate for job opportunities they want and deserve. You have to make your value visible in a currency that has value to the person you want to negotiate with. Jo Miller devotes an entire chapter to this challenge and offers practical advice, with clear examples, of how women leaders can use their accomplishments to make their value visible to get what they want and deserve.

—**Deborah M. Kolb, PhD**, author of *Negotiating at Work*, named by Time, Inc. as one of the best negotiation books of 2015

If you've ever attended one of Jo's leadership programs, you'll know why she receives off-the-charts reviews. Now, *Woman of Influence* gives professional women everywhere access to her guiding principles for leading with influence.

— **Sarah Alter**, president & CEO of Network of Executive Women

Professional women, especially those in technical roles like me, have a burning desire but an uphill battle to leave a legacy of technical brilliance and integrity. Jo Miller's *Woman of Influence* is a groundbreaking guide that I recommend to all professional women who are ready to take the next step in establishing themselves as leaders, influencers, and role models.

—**Serpil Bayraktar**, distinguished engineer, founder
of Cisco Women in Tech, and global chair of
Women in Science and Engineering at Cisco

If you're just getting started in your career, feel stalled in your current position, or can't figure out what's holding you back, *Woman of Influence* is the book for you. I have seen Jo Miller's work transform the lives of countless women for over 15 years—and this book lays out the exact tools you need to become the leader you were meant to be.

—**Deanna Kosaraju**, founder and CEO of
Global Tech Women

Jo's leadership programs have made a remarkable impact for women leaders at MetLife. Now, with the advice laid out in the pages of *Woman of Influence*, anyone can advance their careers thanks to her expertise and wisdom.

—**Rabih Haber**, head of human resources of MetLife
Europe, Middle East, Africa, and Asia-Pacific

Woman of Influence is a must-have guidebook to leading at the next level. Buy this book for your emerging leaders and accelerate their transformation.

—**Olivia Shen Green**, head of diversity and
inclusion of Logitech

There's never been a better time for women to step up and provide authentic, no-nonsense leadership. This guide is packed with practical exercises to bring out the best in you and take your leadership skills to the next level. Whether you're starting out or approaching the C-suite, Jo's insights will help you develop into the leader you aspire to be.

—**Jen Dalitz**, CEO of Women in
Banking & Finance Inc. (Australia)

Woman of Influence is a must-read for any woman who wants to thrive as a leader. No matter where you are in your career, Jo's advice will help you become a more dynamic leader—and have others recognize all that you bring to the table.

—**Tonya Hoopes**, managing partner of Hoopes Events and former executive director of the National Association of Women MBAs

At all stages of their careers, women face strong headwinds in their path to leadership due to systemic barriers. Based on her decades of experience developing women leaders at all stages of their careers, Jo Miller shares the strategies she has seen be most effective—with a sense of humor and playfulness that will woo the reader.

—**Caroline Simard, PhD**, managing director of VMware Women's Leadership Innovation Lab of Stanford University

When our organization is seeking tactical authentic leadership development for women, Jo is at the top of our list. Her work to clearly identify and support pathways to leadership is critically important as we look to advance women leaders at all levels.

—**Tiffany O'Donnell**, CEO of Women Lead Change

Too many books are big on talk and short on action. Jo's book is a practical cookbook for aspiring leaders with all the recipes they need for success.

—**Jeannie Gardner**, GM of the Center of Excellence for Shell and National President of Women's Energy Network (2016–2017)

Jo inspires you to be proud of your authentic self rather than trying to become a prototypical, one-size-fits-all leader. You can become more successful doing more of what you love. Her step-by-step approach teaches you how to find your strength and how to market it.

—**Maureen Fan**, CEO and cofounder of 6-time Emmy winning Baobab Studios

This book is for talented women waiting for their potential and accomplishments to be noticed and rewarded. In this book, Jo Miller offers great advice and exercises to help you raise your own game to the next level of leadership.

—**JoAnna Garcia Sohovich**, CEO of
The Chamberlain Group, Inc.

There's power in surrounding yourself with people who see the leader in you. A strong network of supporters is key to accomplishing amazing things and in this book, Jo shows how to shift your mindset and rebalance where you focus your attention in favor of more leading, less doing.

—**Georgene Huang**, CEO and cofounder of
Fairygodboss

Claiming your value starts with understanding where your power comes from. This book is packed with practical techniques for establishing credibility, growing your influence, and asserting yourself as a leader.

—**Sarah McCrary**, CEO of GasBuddy

Whether you're returning to work after a hiatus, or launching yourself to the next career level, Jo inspires you to think deeply about the kind of leader you want to be and gives you the springboard to get there.

—**Carol Fishman Cohen**, cofounder of iRelaunch

This book is like getting career advice from your best girlfriend. Jo tells it to you straight, but also gives you the tools you need to evolve your leadership to the next level. Every working woman would benefit greatly from reading *Woman of Influence*. If you want to be educated, entertained, and inspired, pick this book up!

—**Iesha Berry**, human resource and
diversity & inclusion executive

WOMAN
of
INFLUENCE

WOMAN
of
INFLUENCE

*9 Steps to Build Your
Brand, Establish Your
Legacy, and Thrive*

JO MILLER

NEW YORK CHICAGO SAN FRANCISCO ATHENS LONDON
MADRID MEXICO CITY MILAN NEW DELHI
SINGAPORE SYDNEY TORONTO

1 2 3 4 5 6 7 8 9   QVS   24 23 22 21 20 19

ISBN   978-1-260-45883-1
MHID   1-260-45883-0

e-ISBN   978-1-260-45884-8
e-MHID   1-260-45884-9

Design by Mauna Eichner and Lee Fukui

Library of Congress Cataloging-in-Publication Data

Names: Miller, Jo (Jo Kay), author.
Title: Woman of influence : 9 steps to build your brand, establish your
   legacy, and thrive / Jo Miller.
Description: New York : McGraw-Hill Education, [2020] | Includes
   bibliographical references and index.
Identifiers: LCCN 2019031886 (print) | LCCN 2019031887 (ebook) | ISBN
   9781260458831 (hardcover) | ISBN 9781260458848 (ebook)
Subjects: LCSH: Businesswomen. | Leadership in women. | Women--Vocational
   guidance.
Classification: LCC HF5382.6 .M55 2020 (print) | LCC HF5382.6 (ebook) |
   DDC 658.4/09082--dc23
LC record available at https://lccn.loc.gov/2019031886
LC ebook record available at https://lccn.loc.gov/2019031887

Be Leaderly™ is a trademark of Be Leaderly, Inc.
Illustrations by Marichiel Boudwin.

McGraw-Hill Education books are available at special quantity discounts to use as premiums and sales promotions or for use in corporate training programs. To contact a representative, please visit the Contact Us pages at www.mhprofessional.com.

Contents

Introduction

Reinvent Yourself as a
Woman of Influence

Over the past 20 years, I've been on a mission to help women step into the leadership pipeline and thrive.

A lot has changed during that time. Through movements like #MeToo, national marches, and office walkouts, women are speaking up in record numbers—and many organizations are starting to listen. Despite this changing landscape, women still aren't achieving career advancement comparable to men's. You already know this. We've all read the stats.

Professional women at all career levels continue to tell me that they feel stalled and don't know what specifically to do to move ahead in their organization. The struggle is real. You're not alone if you're tired of being told you need to lean in, fix yourself, stop being so aggressive, take one for the team, or wait patiently for your organization to change.

You deserve nothing less than a lifetime of work that plays to your strengths, energizes you, and allows you to operate at your best every day, without being anything other than your authentic, luminous self.

I believe everyone has a personal mission, a reason for being on this planet. Mine: to give women, like you, a clear and proven plan for how to step into the leadership pipeline and present yourself as the talented leader you are.

My purpose in writing this book is to help you develop a career where you can make a meaningful impact doing work that is rewarding and impeccably suited to your talents—and makes your heart sing. It's not too much to ask for.

CLOSING THE PERCEPTION GAP

"I feel like I'm the best-kept secret in this organization," said Tina.*

Tina was a whip-smart corporate finance analyst with a killer work ethic—and by no means an entry-level employee. But as the youngest, most recent addition to her team before an 18-month hiring freeze, she struggled to shrug off the perception that she was the "junior" one in the group.

Tina's role involved detailed monitoring of and reporting on company investment accounts. The work meshed with her strengths, and she got it done quickly. She came in every day, crushed it, and looked for what to do next. Eager to show she could take on more (and be a valuable team player), Tina offered to assist some senior managers with anything they needed help with.

Care to guess what happened next?

The senior managers figured out that they could dump low-priority tasks onto Tina, who got so buried under a mountain of busywork that no one got to see her sophisticated analytical and problem-solving skills.

When I met Tina, she asked for some coaching and explained that it filled her with anxiety to imagine being stuck for another 18 months in a role where she felt underutilized and saw no chance of growth. "I feel like I'm the invisible employee," she said.

She'd become indispensable for doing work that hid her potential.

"What personal brand are you known for today?" I asked. Tina's eyes widened. "I'm the pooper-scooper!" she said, and she spoke of rolling up her sleeves to clean up all kinds of messes that nobody else wanted to bother with. "That's not much of a leadership brand," I said, and we both laughed.

We made an inventory of her technical strengths and the raw leadership strengths that were going unseen. Tina made a list of ways she could see herself making a larger impact that would generate wins for her team and add value to her company. We discussed steps she could take to close the gap between what she was capable of and how others perceived her.

---

* All stories and quotes are from conversations conducted by the author, unless accompanied by a citation. If only a first name is used, it's a pseudonym to respect the person's privacy.

Tina described how she wanted to use her analytical skills to identify critical business issues, propose solutions, and make sure those solutions were implemented. Not only that, but she also wanted ensure the changes would stick. Soon, Tina was bursting with enthusiasm for what was possible. "I see myself as a change agent," she said.

And just like that, Tina reinvented how she saw herself. She immediately began to think and act more like a change agent than a newbie. She diplomatically informed her colleagues that she was no longer accepting pooper-scooper tasks, and she worked with her manager to identify some problems that were worthy of attention from an analytical problem solver and change agent. Tina was so successful with her first two projects that she became known as *the* change agent on her team. She was promoted within a year, and she began helping junior team members to get clear on their value too.

Let's face it: it isn't always easy to break out and establish yourself as an up-and-coming leader.

Perhaps you have developed a great reputation as a valuable contributor with a solid work ethic, but you wonder why it's not translating into career advancement. Maybe you saw a coveted role get snapped up by a colleague—a job you know you could crush, if given the chance. Or maybe you raised your hand for a promotion, only to be told you're not strategic enough, or not ready yet, or that you lack "executive presence" (whatever the heck that is) despite the fact that you're already doing the work. If any of this sounds like you, I want to be clear: you're not alone.

> **Let's face it: it isn't always easy to break out and establish yourself as an up-and-coming leader.**

WHAT'S HOLDING YOU BACK?

I've spent over two decades helping women develop their leadership skills, and I'm honored that 100,000 professional women have dedicated time to their development by attending my workshops, webinars, and coaching programs. They have taught me about their strengths, passions, and aspirations, and they've confided the roadblocks, frustrations, and insults they've endured.

Along the way, I identified three distinct ways women often get bogged down on the path to realizing our leadership potential—situations that prevent us from being the leaders that we're capable of becoming. See if one of them resonates with you.

You're More of a Leader Than You Think

I frequently watch women be unaware of how much they already are a leader. Their internal monologue whispers, "But I'm not a leader yet," when in fact they have bucketloads of leadership ability.

Research proves this is a misperception. A gobsmacking 72 percent of managers have the raw talent to continue advancing toward C-level roles, but their companies are letting a wealth of leadership talent go unacknowledged and undeveloped.[1] It's entirely possible your leadership strengths are hiding in plain sight.

If you relate to this challenge, this book will help you recognize how competent you already are by identifying your existing leadership style and strengths and uncovering the unique value you bring to your organization. This knowledge will enable and embolden you to seize opportunities to prove this competence to others—and to yourself.

You're the Best-Kept Secret in Your Organization

I've also come into contact with many women who *are* confidently making a large impact as a leader, but they are struggling to close the gap between what they bring to the table and how others perceive them.

As I will explain in Chapter 4, this perception gap persists among 70 percent of women leaders, even those at the top of their organizations.[2]

If this sounds like you, we'll work together to sharply define your leadership niche, so you can wield it like a superpower and cut through the noise to become visible and appreciated.

You're Too Busy Leading to Focus on Your Future

I've met women who feel their leadership skills are being utilized and appreciated.

They're moving mountains on behalf of their organizations, but that can be all-consuming, at a cost to their personal aspirations.

Only 30 percent of established women leaders are happy with how they're perceived in their organizations and feel it fully reflects their true leadership potential.[3] If this is you, you may want to make the most of this moment and capitalize on it to further your career.

Being indispensable in your current job won't move your career forward. Your first step is to give yourself permission to pause, so you can revisit and reimagine what you want for yourself and apply what you know about business strategy to your career strategy. Then give your personal brand a tune-up, so it communicates your long-term potential, and use that insight to take on assignments to grow on your own terms.

> **Being indispensable in your current job won't move your career forward.**

A ROADMAP FOR REINVENTION

Through my company, Be Leaderly, I've surveyed more than 3,000 professionals, the majority of whom were women, and I've interviewed more than 150 executive women about the factors that contributed to their career and leadership development.[4] From those conversations and surveys, I learned how they stood up for their strengths and used them to blaze an uncompromising path into leadership. One thing's clear: you can do the same.

Backed by all I have learned, I reverse engineered a step-by-step process for you to reinvent yourself as a woman of influence and thrive in that role. I'll show how to bridge the gap between where you are in your career and your leadership aspirations, with stories and mindset shifts to provide you with new inspiration and determination. I reinforce those lessons by laying out concrete actions to take, using a blend of self-assessments, practical exercises, and checklists that have been road tested by tens of thousands of my workshop participants. I also show how to avoid 12 common, highly relatable career missteps made by even the most savvy aspiring leaders. Each misstep is paired with a Leaderly Move—a career-accelerating leadership step to take instead.

The steps are pragmatic and proven, with specific strategies and tools you can use to accomplish the following:

- **Identify and clearly articulate your value** and why it matters to your organization—and use that knowledge to advance your career
- **"Up-level" your personal brand into a leadership brand** and promote it in a way that persuades your organization to sit up and pay attention
- **Cultivate a well-rounded, supportive network** of collaborators and influencers who appreciate your value and can connect you to new career and leadership opportunities

Before I share the steps themselves, there are a few things to know about how to make the most of this book.

BOOK, MEET LIFE

I know what it's like to pick up a book that makes big promises but is completely unrealistic to implement. Some weeks, simply finding time to read critical emails, much less open a book, can be a major win. One thing I know for sure from speaking to hundreds of thousands of working women is that the number 1 internal challenge we wrestle with is not lacking self-confidence or innate ability to lead, or neglecting to "lean in." Instead, it's how much we already have crammed onto our plates. Don't worry though. You're in good company if the demands placed on your time and energy often feel overwhelming—and this book will reveal some solutions.

We rarely allow ourselves the gift of pausing in the midst of everything that's going on in life to evaluate and ask: "Am I on the right trajectory?" You don't have to be a rocket scientist to know that a minor boost or course correction can completely alter your path.

So I'm also going to ask you to pause at times and complete exercises that will apply the concepts in the book to your life. I encourage you not to skip them. They build on each other, and I recommend taking notes in whatever way is easiest for you—whether it's on paper, in a journal, or in a notes app. There are also worksheets at www.jomiller.com/womanof influence that you can download and print. When you see a section titled "Own It," expect to find questions to ask yourself, things to think about, or other actions to take.

Some of these activities might feel like work—time-guzzling, effort-consuming work, especially in Part 1 (Chapters 1 to 3)—but each step is necessary for establishing yourself as a confident, sought-after leader.

If you need to pick the book up and put it down, check in and check out, that's OK, as long as you stick with the process. As you move from Part I to Parts II (Chapters 4 to 7) and III (Chapters 8 and 9), you'll notice a transition to actions you can incorporate into things you'd otherwise be doing during the course of a workday or week.

Plus, becoming a leader is not about adding more to a to-do list that's already longer than a CVS receipt. Leadership is not about *doing* more. It's about switching from *doing* to *leading* and transforming that to-do list into a *to-lead* list. Chapter 5 pairs this mindset shift with an exercise to identify activities to let go of, so you can do more leading. In the same spirit, some Own It exercises include an Outsource It option, in case it's more achievable to enlist support from others or if your learning style is "talk it out" rather than write it out.

> **Leadership is not about *doing* more. It's about switching from *doing* to *leading*.**

This is your real life, and as you know, life can be complicated and messy, but you muddle through and do your best. It's like when you're working from home because your kid, parent, or pet can't stop throwing up. You're about to dial into a teleconference when you realize—holy Zoom, Batwoman—*it's a videoconference*. One minute later, you're good to go with a rumpled jacket, swipe of distractingly bright lipstick, and webcam angled away from the laundry pile. You beam at the customer and kick off the meeting. #Winning.

You know your constraints better than anyone, and so all I'm asking you to do is show up and give this all you've got in the time you have available.

Hang in there with me. Don't skimp on the initial steps. Move through those and we'll move on to the high-visibility, high-reward stuff you're here for.

The prize to keep your eye on is gaining a deep understanding of what you have to offer and the work you're best suited to. That way, you can attract and accept assignments that align with your leadership strengths and aspirations, attack the big meaty problems only you can solve, and not waste time struggling to execute work that's someone else's forte, not yours.

> **The prize to keep your eye on is gaining a deep understanding of what you have to offer and the work you're best suited to.**

HERE'S WHAT TO EXPECT

The book is laid out with nine clear, practical steps you can take to become the most "leaderly" version of yourself possible. Each step has its own chapter.

In Part I, "Advancing Authentically," I'll help you see yourself as a leader, now, without changing who you are. You'll also answer the key question **"Who am I as a leader?"** as you tackle the first three chapters and steps:

- *Chapter 1, Put on Your Big Girl Pants.* You don't need a title to be a leader or to accomplish amazing things. Learn about five types of leaders, none that require a team of people to report to you, and recognize which of the roles you're best suited to playing.
- *Chapter 2, You Do You.* Your professional, leadership, and character strengths are your most powerful differentiators. Find out how to spot yours, at any career stage.
- *Chapter 3, What's Your Superpower?* To claim your leadership niche, connect the dots from your strengths to work you love to do and that is also a valuable asset to your organization.

In Part II, "Building an Influential Brand," I'll walk you step-by-step through a real-world guide to reimagining your personal brand and promoting it in a way that makes everyone around you sit up, pay attention, and see the leader in you. You'll address the key question **"How can I change how others perceive me as a leader?"** as you move through Chapters 4 to 7:

- *Chapter 4, Boss Up Your Brand.* Everyone has a brand. Most people have one by default, but yours should be built by design, or it may stifle your career growth. You'll craft a personal brand statement that stands for something bigger than you can accomplish alone—and lands like "bam."
- *Chapter 5, Get Your Shift Together.* If you aspire to make big things happen and move beyond your current role, you need to think and act less like a doer and more like a leader. Find out how shifting your mindset from "me" to "we" can have instant results.
- *Chapter 6, Go Big or Go Home.* The stakes can be high, but a well-chosen, high-profile role or stretch assignment can be career defining, and it can propel you to new heights. And the opportunities you say no to will be just as important as those you accept.
- *Chapter 7, Amplify Your Accomplishments.* It's a myth that work speaks for itself. Learn effective ways to make your leadership brand and key accomplishments visible, without feeling awkward or inauthentic.

In Part III, "Mobilizing Your Support Squad," we'll wrap the book up with practical steps and insights on building an influential network of collaborators and allies. You'll answer the key question **"Whose help can I enlist?"** as you forge ahead through the last two chapters:

- *Chapter 8, Rally Your Crew.* Deep personal relationships, not large superficial networks, are the foundation of leadership. People don't follow a title. They follow someone they trust. A well-rounded, supportive, and influential network requires the four types of people described in this chapter.
- *Chapter 9, Attract Influential Advocates.* If there's a closed door between you and your next career breakthrough, having the backing of influential sponsors can make all the difference. Learn what sponsorship is, why you're underestimating its value, and why you can't ask for it, although you can up your chances to earn it.

Now that you have a map for closing the gap between where you are and your leadership aspirations, let's get to work.

WOMAN
of
INFLUENCE

Advancing Authentically

PART I

We are often so focused on trying to fix our weaknesses that we neglect to nurture our passions and strengths. In Part I we'll take the opposite approach so you can authentically and accurately answer the question "Who am I as a leader?"

- **Chapter 1, Put on Your Big Girl Pants: Lead from Where You Are.** You don't need a title to be a leader. This chapter will help you see yourself as a leader—now, without changing who you are—and gain insight into your intrinsic leadership type.

- **Chapter 2, You Do You: Own Your Leadership Strengths.** Who are you as a leader, really? The answer lies in understanding your professional, leadership, and character strengths and shining a spotlight on these powerful differentiators.

- **Chapter 3, What's Your Superpower? Claim Your Leadership Niche.** Once you identify your signature leadership strengths, the work you love to do, and the value you bring to your organization, you can claim a unique and distinctive leadership niche.

Put on Your Big Girl Pants

Lead from Where You Are

> *Leadership is an action, not a position.*
> —Cindy Pace

There are an overwhelming number of leadership books and gurus devoted to answering the question: What is leadership?

I love the definition that I learned many years ago from a telecommunications engineer. In a preworkshop survey I had asked: "Why is being a leader important to you?" The engineer responded that being a leader was not all that important to her. She simply wanted to come to work every day and make the biggest possible difference she could. I won't lie: I was underwhelmed at first by her response. Then it hit me, like BOOM:

**Leadership is making a bigger difference
than you can make alone.**

That's it.

When you take this definition to heart, you don't need a title to be a leader, and you don't need to head up a team to accomplish remarkable things. By this definition, you're probably already a leader. To lead means to engage, inspire, influence, and motivate others to collaborate with you to make something great happen, together. This is what I mean when

5

I refer to being "leaderly," and it's fast becoming an essential skill at any job level.

These days, 84 percent of employees are *matrixed*, meaning they work with a range of people from multiple teams and receive instructions from more than one manager.[1] As more work gets done across teams and across functions, people typically become more collaborative but less clear on what's actually expected of them. In this environment, leaders who rely on positional authority alone are being supplanted by people who can lead effectively regardless of their formal role.

> To lead means to engage, inspire, influence, and motivate others to collaborate with you to make something great happen, together.

The necessity of this skill never goes away. Senior executives influence their peers. CEOs influence their board. Leaders at all levels routinely find themselves needing to influence without any real authority in terms of reporting relationships.

"There are very few roles today that have 'command and control' type authority. Most require leading with influence, the most powerful form of leadership," says Holly Meidl, vice president of risk services for Ascension, a large healthcare provider. "All organizations need leaders at every job level and are looking for those who will step up and lead."

RECOGNIZE THE LEADER IN YOURSELF

Dr. Cindy Pace would be the first to admit that she wasn't always purposeful about lobbying for leadership roles. Cindy, a global talent and diversity leader, says a defining moment arose early in her career when she was unexpectedly thrust into a highly visible leadership role.

When Cindy's colleague became ill while planning a global conference for 200 people, Cindy received an unexpected visit from her manager. "My boss came into my office for one of those 'put on your big girl pants' conversations and said, 'Cindy, I need your help.'" He had noticed and appreciated how much Cindy was contributing behind the scenes, but the situation had changed. He wanted to know, could she step up and lead the conference?

In that moment, though she was feeling somewhat terrified, Cindy had the self-awareness to realize, "Someone sees the leader in me. I should be seeing the leader in me too." Cindy accepted the assignment, and the experiences and exposure that came with it changed everything for her. It was a turning point in her career and how she saw herself as a leader. Prior to that push, says Cindy, "I did not realize how much I was dancing around the daisies. I was not really stepping up to lead."

When people see the leader in you, don't let them down. Trust what they see, and learn to see the leader in yourself.

Since then, Cindy has been focused on unapologetically unleashing her leadership potential and coaching others to do the same. Now, in her day job, Cindy is vice president, global chief diversity and inclusion officer, with one of the world's largest insurance firms. Picture a globe-trotting human dynamo who travels the world, calling for women to step into the leadership pipeline.

> **When people see the leader in you, don't let them down. Trust what they see, and learn to see the leader in yourself.**

MISSTEP 1

Waiting for permission or an invitation to be a leader is Misstep 1 in the list of 12 career derailers (which are listed in the Appendix at the end of the book) that might be putting a lid on your ability to rise.

Each time I mention a misstep, I'll highlight a Leaderly Move—a courageous, career-accelerating step you can take instead. This one is *recognizing the leader in yourself.* "See yourself as a leader now," says Cindy. "Leadership is an action, not a position."

THE RAW TRUTH ABOUT RAW TALENT

Lean in close so I can whisper a secret in your ear:

> **Raw leadership talent isn't nearly as rare as you've been led to believe.**

When researchers with the executive search firm Egon Zhender studied the attributes of managers from thousands of organizations, they found that 72 percent had the raw talent to make it into C-suite roles.[2] The biggest problem: Employers haven't figured out how to fully develop prospective leaders, which limits how far those managers advance. Leadership *talent* isn't rare, but leadership *development* is.

This statistic confirmed two things I've long known deep in my gut and that I've spent the last two decades obsessing over:

1. No one should be shy about raising her hand to be developed as a leader.
2. No one is going to take charge of your leadership development the way you can and must.

The catch is that developing as a leader is not about *changing* yourself. It's about *becoming* yourself.

So as you learn and grow, stay anchored in your natural leadership style, strengths, and what you can uniquely contribute. Give yourself permission to show up as you are and grow from there.

When you emulate someone else's style, you cancel out your own. You'll likely feel like an imposter, and that's no way to lead boldly and effectively.

TINY ACTS OF LEADERSHIP

There's an entire industry of books and seminars founded on the assumption that if you just learn the right set skills and behaviors, you'll be a leader (though which skills those are, few seem to agree on). I'm here to tell you there's an easier way.

Pay attention to your *existing* leadership behaviors.

I'll never forget a conversation I had with the head of research and development for a company that designs networking equipment. She said there isn't any role in a company today that isn't a leadership position and that every time you interact with your fellow workers, you have the opportunity to commit what she called "acts of leadership."

Acts of leadership can be as simple as these:

- Asking an insightful question that reconnects your team back to its strategy
- Acknowledging someone who's doing the right but difficult thing
- Encouraging a group to reach for a goal that's slightly beyond what's comfortable
- Calling out someone for her grit when she's having a train wreck of a day
- Reminding people that change can be hard, so hang in there
- Attacking the strategic task before the easy task
- Saying "Let her finish" when someone's getting talked over
- Voicing agreement in support of a great point made by a colleague

Your days are filled with opportunities to take the lead.

Pay attention to the moments when you make a bigger impact through others than you can make alone—and galvanize bystanders, enticing them to become followers. You'll see people sit up a little straighter, lean in a bit closer, and listen more intently. They'll light up, ask questions, and offer to pitch in.

You've probably heard the time-honored management tip "Catch people doing something right." In the next Own It exercise, you'll practice *catching yourself leading something right*, however small. Doing this will help reveal your "leadership catnip"—that is, your leadership strengths that others find irresistible. Whether you own it or outsource it, afterward think about what you learned about your natural leadership strengths.

Sharpen your instincts by calling attention to others as they commit acts of leadership too. You'll start to notice leadership *everywhere* once you look for it, and you'll also prove to yourself and your squad how much of a leader you already are.

OWN IT

Identify Your Leadership Catnip

Note: This is the first Own It exercise. Answers from these exercises will often build on each other, so consider keeping your answers together in one place. If you have a hard copy of the book, go ahead and write in the margins or keep a journal nearby. If it's an e-book, use a notes app or a notebook. You can also find worksheets and other resources for you at www.jomiller.com/womanofinfluence.

Acts of leadership others find irresistible make up your leadership catnip. Here's how to discover yours:

- **Observe yourself leading.** For at least a couple of days, pay attention when you interact with other people and look for any instance in which you make a bigger impact than you could have made by yourself. Every action counts, big or small, in person or virtually.

- **Document what you see.** Keep a running list of each time you catch yourself leading. Be generous in your self-assessment.

- **Look for themes.** Review the list and see if you can detect any recurring leadership strengths.

- **Create more leaderly moments.** Based on those insights, look out for more opportunities to commit acts of leadership.

OUTSOURCE IT

Identify Your Leadership Catnip

Note: Some exercises, like this one, will include an Outsource It option, in case you prefer to enlist support from others or if you learn by "talking it out."

- **Enlist an observer.** If you would benefit from an outside perspective, enlist help from someone who knows you well. A good candidate is an observant colleague who tends to see the good in people. Offer to return the favor.

- **Describe the objective.** Explain that leadership means *making a bigger difference than you can make alone.* Ask your helper to monitor you and note any leadership behaviors she spots, large and small.

- **Exchange observations.** Meet up for coffee, macarons, and a debriefing.

DON'T BE A PROFESSIONAL PRETZEL

I started my career in sales. After college, I landed my dream job at a boutique staffing agency for creative freelancers, and I desperately wanted to succeed at it. But I quickly felt like I was twisting myself into pretzel-like knots, trying to become someone who wasn't really me at all.

I was an introvert trying to act like an extrovert, a daydreamer and conceptual thinker floundering in a business development role. That particular job did not end well—in fact, I got fired. Rather than interpret that as feedback, I hustled my way into *another* similar role. Thankfully, that experience led me to the work I do today as a leadership trainer and fiercely committed advocate for women in leadership. It's a vastly better match for my natural strengths.

Trying to be someone you're not can be exhausting. The alternative is to craft a career that capitalizes on your strengths and allows you to bring your authentic self to work.

> **Trying to be someone you're not can be exhausting. The alternative is to craft a career that capitalizes on your strengths and allows you to bring your authentic self to work.**

11

The idea of being unabashedly yourself at work may seem daunting, especially if you're early in your career, and potentially exhausting in its own way too. But I can tell you from experience, it's anything but.

When I stopped fighting against my innate abilities and began exploiting them instead, it opened doors to discovering *different* strengths that I never knew I had. Backed by a series of influential mentors, I took a leap and pivoted into my new career. Today, I am CEO of Be Leaderly, a leadership development, consulting, and research firm dedicated to amplifying women's voices at work. I ultimately ended up in a much more awesome job—and I have been more successful at it—than I ever could have daydreamed.

Being a leader doesn't require changing who you are. In fact, authentic leaders have happier followers, so it *is* possible to advance your career while remaining true to yourself and being recognized for your unique gifts.[3]

THERE'S MORE THAN ONE TYPE OF LEADER. WHICH ONE ARE YOU?

McKinsey & Company discovered that effective leaders share four behaviors that account for nearly 90 percent of leadership effectiveness:

- Supporting others
- Solving problems
- Seeking out different perspectives
- Delivering results[4]

While these activities form a baseline of what any effective leader must do, how you do them is *entirely up to you.*

I was at a biotech company's leadership retreat for high-potential women, leading the group through an exercise to develop a personal brand statement as an inspiring and engaging emerging leader. (We'll do this in Chapter 4.) One of the participants asked a couple of questions I hear often: "Can anyone be a leader? Do you have to manage people in order to be a leader?" Vice President and General Manager Amy Butler replied: "There's more than one type of leader. You need to figure out which one you are." That's *your* next task.

A *leadership brand statement* melds your strengths, passions, impact, and aspirations into a single, succinct expression—a tiny but mighty declaration of who you are and what you stand for. I share 50 of my favorite examples in Chapter 4. As I curated that list, grouping like with like, I noticed that they fell into five general categories (in alphabetical order):

1. **Change leaders** make organizations better, through disrupting, transforming, and optimizing them.
2. **People leaders** thrive on developing people, teams, and organizational cultures.
3. **Results leaders** are goal driven and motivated to strive for a high bar of performance.
4. **Service leaders** fight to support others, whether external customers, internal stakeholders, or a certain population, and see them succeed.
5. **Thought leaders** are the experts, visionaries, and futuristic thinkers who love to innovate and disseminate knowledge.

Organizations need them all, but somehow word got around that people leaders are the only type worthy of the title "leader." This could not be more wrong.

There's nothing quite like being in a room full of people who have just internalized the truthbomb that not everyone needs to be, or should be, a people leader. Those who recognize that particular leadership style as their own glow with pride, knowing that they have a special gift. Everyone else emits a palpable sense of relief at no longer having to pretend to be or want to be people leaders. They too can embrace their strengths.

Internalizing what you're good at and what you're not good at is liberating. Personally, I like to think of myself as a thought leader and a subject-matter expert. My team at Be Leaderly includes a terrific service leader and an inspirational thought leader. Thankfully, they're both also great at leading themselves, which compensates for the fact that I'm not a people leader. Reminder: You don't need to have people reporting to you to be a leader. All of the examples I'm about to share come from different types of leaders who have all made great things happen without managing a team.

Change Leaders

Change leaders are strategizers, optimizers, and roadblock removers. They take large, complex business goals that can't be achieved by an organization in its current state and lead transformation so the goal becomes possible. They eliminate inefficiencies and break down barriers that others fail to see.

Kathy Tyra once worked at a company that kept having problems with either too much inventory or not enough. Kathy, now vice president of workplace resources and real estate with a tech company, saw the mounting delays and costs and decided there had to be a better way. She worked with vendors to come up with a plan to streamline the materials pipeline without causing delays to customers, and she spent a good deal of time thinking through how it would work. She solicited input from coworkers, leaders, customers, and suppliers, and she delivered presentations to communicate the idea. "Because I used a collaborative process, everyone felt ownership for making the implementation a success," she says.

Signs that you're a **change leader**:

- You can't help but spot improvements that could make life easier for your customers or team.
- You love to attack a stretch goal by changing underlying conditions and mindsets that could be preventing the goal from being realized.
- You have a passion for excellence and are always looking for a smarter, faster, more efficient way to get things done.

People Leaders

People leaders take time to understand others, identifying their strengths and exploring what motivates them. They build people up and help them grow. They also ensure that the right people are in the right roles and everyone's working together as a team, focused on a common goal.

"Our team had a technology project to complete that was new for all of us," says Ann Finkner, senior vice president and chief administrative officer for Farm Credit Services of America. Reflecting on a time when she held an individual contributor role, she explained that most people on the team didn't know where to start or even what needed to get done. Not knowing the answers either, Ann offered to lead the project on behalf of the team. The project's success required not only understanding the new technology but also educating and engaging her teammates. "It became a catalyst for my career to evolve into higher-level leadership," says Ann.

When I asked Ann about the traits she now most appreciates seeing in aspiring people leaders in her organization, she described how they artfully blend personal risk taking with patience, teamwork, and collaboration. Their standout skills include listening, asking good questions, and being inquisitive.

Signs that you're a **people leader**:

- You enjoy motivating, empowering, and developing people.
- You give credit to others and recognize people who do great work.
- Your greatest joy is seeing others succeed.

Results Leaders

Results leaders are attracted to audacious targets and will do what it takes to achieve them. They are ambitious, persistent, and tenacious "goal-getters" who enjoy celebrating success and recognizing others when they win. This type of leader has a knack for interpersonal influence and rallying others around a challenging goal. "I always make my number," says one results-oriented operations leader who has never been in charge of a large team or a big budget but knows how to enlist support from across her organization.

Alice Katwan is now senior vice president of North America sales at Salesforce, but her first sales role was at Montgomery Ward, where she sold drapes and blinds. She was the top salesperson. Never mind that she was only part time and still in high school.

Alice loved being able to objectively measure and track her performance. "I have always liked being able to know where I stand at all times," she says. "No one can argue with the numbers." Later, working her way through college, Alice sold faucets and toilets for a kitchen and bathroom supplier, where again she was the top salesperson. Her results-oriented drive gave her a sense of job security. "Because I exceeded my monthly sales targets, I was able to focus on school instead of worrying about whether I was doing a good job."

Signs that you're a **results leader**:

- You get fired up by having clear, meaningful, measurable goals and unleashing the competitive spirit in others.
- You thrive in competitive work environments.
- When faced with a demanding goal that might make others crumple, you say "watch me."

Service Leaders

Service leaders are fueled by fierce determination to make life better or easier for people—whether they're clients, consumers, or even human-kind. They champion the products, services, solutions, or experiences that customers love. They see themselves as partners, advocates, and ac-tivists. They have the uncanny ability to step into another's shoes, com-prehend that person's situation, and channel that empathy into solutions and tangible change. Service leaders were the rarest leadership type among those I surveyed. Our world needs more of them.

Liz Brenner, a former vice president of human resources, counts customer-centric thinking as one of her most deeply ingrained core values. Years ago, Liz was asked to develop a unified digital marketing strategy for her company's services. Each service had its own marketing person or team, and all were vocal about why their agenda mattered most. Liz put on her "customer hat" to push for a more holistic view and corralled her peer group to speak with one voice. Says Liz, "We often get so involved in our day-to-day work that we lose sight of the big picture and who we are trying to serve." She went on to take increasingly customer-centric roles, at first championing the cause of external customers and later her com-pany's employees.

Signs that you're a **service leader**:

- You side with your customers, elevate their voice, and champion their cause.
- Your values and personal mission come alive in your work.
- Your purpose is to stand up for others and help them thrive.

Thought Leaders

"Thought leaders are the trusted opinion leaders and go-to people in their fields of expertise," says Denise Brosseau, author of *Ready to Be a Thought Leader?* They are more than just "ideas" people. "They galvanize and inspire others with innovative ideas and help them scale those ideas into sustainable change," says Denise. They build deep, specialized expertise in an area they're passionate about. They work to stay on trend with new developments, and they contribute game-changing breakthroughs to their field, cause, or industry.

Nina Bhatti, PhD, is CEO of Kokko. Early in her career as a researcher and technologist, her employer signed a deal with an important customer, promising cutting-edge innovations that no other supplier could deliver. There was just one problem. "Nobody knew what that meant, and people were scared," says Nina, who holds 24 patents and invented the first accurate color-matching system that worked on smartphones. She raised her hand and asked to lead the project. As she listened to her customers describe their challenges, Nina realized they wanted to move into the mobile space. She went on to contribute new mobile-computing technologies and build first-of-a-kind solutions.

Signs that you're a **thought leader**:

- You're passionate about your area of expertise, have a thirst for learning, and love to share your knowledge with others.
- You're always looking for ways to apply your knowledge to make a difference.
- You light up when you discover a challenging problem to solve.

Are You a Mashup?

If you're thinking, "I don't fit neatly into any of those boxes," that's OK. All of the lists and categories I've shared are here to inspire you, not limit you. Every leader needs to drive change, engage and empower others, deliver results, make a positive impact, and generate big ideas. You'll hopscotch across the boundaries every day. The question is which you're most at home with and what role really makes you light up.

You're not necessarily born into one category where you remain for life. Some of the leaders I interviewed started out kicking butt as one leadership type, then switched to another as their strengths and situational demands changed. For instance, Nina's early success as a thought leader on her high-profile customer innovation project got her promoted into her first business leadership role, where she oversaw technical teams. She's now a startup CEO.

Though your style will undoubtedly evolve as your career progresses, it's useful to identify one type to focus on as your immediate pathway forward. The next exercise will help you identify whether you're primarily a change, people, results, service, or thought leader.

OWN IT

Which Type of Leader Are You?

Reflect on the five leadership types—change, people, results, service, or thought— and think about which one you relate to the most. As you review the signs to look for, note any you strongly identify with. Ask yourself, "Where does my primary motivation come from?" From there, select the role that suits you best.

OUTSOURCE IT

Which Type of Leader Are You?

Show the list of five types of leaders to a handful of people who know you well. Ask: "Am I best suited to being a change, people, results, service, or thought leader?"

CHAPTER 1 WRAP-UP

So far, we've established that you don't need a title to be a leader or to make great things happen. You learned about the five leadership types, none of which require you to have a team of people reporting to you or to fundamentally change who you are.

By following the exercises, you've gotten used to catching yourself (and others) in the act of leading, gained some insight into your natural leadership style, and identified whether you're a change, people, results, service, or thought leader.

The next chapter dives deeper into exploring your strengths by segmenting them into three distinct categories, to gain a better understanding of what you bring to the table as a leader that's truly unique.

You Do You

Own Your Leadership Strengths

> *Nobody can be you the way that you can be you. It is your distinct competitive advantage.*[1]
> **—Carla Harris,**
> vice chair, managing director, and senior client advisor, Morgan Stanley

In Chapter 1, you explored how much of a leader you already are by catching yourself in the act of leading—when you make a bigger impact than you can make alone. You discovered your personal "leadership catnip"—those leadership behaviors others find irresistible. And you identified the role you found the most relatable: being a change, people, results, service, or thought leader.

Now, in Chapter 2, you'll answer the question, "Who am I as a leader, really?" The answer lies not in changing who you are but in revealing where you already sparkle. To do this, we'll shine a spotlight on three types of strengths: professional, leadership, and character. These form a platform from which you can lead, rise, and thrive—without selling out your soul.

YOUR STRENGTHS ARE A POWERFUL DIFFERENTIATOR

If you're ready to never again be a professional pretzel, twisting yourself in knots to be something that you're not or your organization's best-kept secret waiting for an opportunity to step up and lead, here's the first step: get as clear as a precision-cut Swarovski crystal on your strengths.

Take it from me, a reformed professional pretzel, that identifying, embracing, employing, and amplifying those strengths can form the foundation of an exhilarating career.

"You grow most in your areas of greatest strength," says Marcus Buckingham, coauthor of *Now, Discover Your Strengths.* "You will improve the most, be the most creative, be the most inquisitive, and bounce back the fastest in those areas where you have already shown some natural advantage over everyone else—your strengths."[2]

To be clear, this doesn't mean being blind to your weaknesses. It means you'll experience greater growth by unapologetically, uncompromisingly throwing yourself at developing in areas you're already strong in.

The benefits of using strengths to shape a career have been widely studied, dissected, and discussed by Marcus and others. But there are some eye-opening facts worth knowing:

- People who use their strengths every day are *three times* more likely to report having an excellent quality of life.[3]
- They are also *six times* more likely to be engaged in their work and enjoy a bump in productivity, and they are less likely to quit.[4]

Despite these benefits, strengths are vastly underleveraged. What percentage of workers do you think get to use their strengths every day?

Take a guess.

The answer: Fewer than 20 percent of people strongly agree that they get to use their strengths every day.[5] Up against these odds, purposefully structuring a career around your strengths can truly set you apart.

MISSTEP 2

Misstep 2 on the list of 12 career-limiting missteps to avoid is *doing work that will never make you shine.*

The Leaderly Move to take in its place is *owning your leadership strengths.* Your strengths are a natural competitive advantage. If you want to stand out, *you do you.*

THE HIGH COST OF WORKING AGAINST YOUR STRENGTHS

Of the surveys I analyzed from more than 1,200 leadership program participants, one of the strongest themes that emerged was a viscerally strong yearning to do work that played to their strengths.[6] Many, it seemed, had firsthand experience with the high cost of doing work that felt like a grind. Perhaps you've had that experience too.

When I asked, "What challenges do you currently face in your career?" many cited the stress of navigating a workplace where their strengths were unknown or undervalued. Here are some of their comments:

- My managers are unaware of my skills, strengths, and goals.
- I need to learn how to showcase my strengths.
- My boss, the president of the company, can see my strengths; however, the other owners do not.
- I would like to move into product management where my communication and big-picture strengths are more valued.
- How can I use my strengths to portray myself as a leader?

Answers to my question, "What are your top career goals for the next three years?" unearthed a strong collective craving to be in a role or on a path to advancement that centered on personal strengths, with goals like these:

- Find ways to integrate my general strengths into my job.
- Learn how to develop my leadership strengths in a way that benefits the business and those I work with.

- Rebuild my confidence in my strengths.
- Be promoted into a position that fits my strengths.
- Get more clarity as to what my strengths are, as well as where I can go in my career. I consider myself a natural leader, and I would like to build upon those skills at work.

One quote that summed all of this up quite beautifully came from a product manager with a digital marketing firm: "I'd like to know how to elevate my game by tapping into my strengths, gaining visibility, getting credit for my accomplishments, and learning how to know when and where to move up or move on," she wrote. (As if to demonstrate the power of declaring such an intention, I learned that seven months later she had moved up into a director-level role.)

Perhaps you have a similar challenge. Maybe your capabilities are unrecognized or misunderstood, or you're on a track that's mismatched to your talents. Or maybe you'd like to discover or further develop your strengths, evolve your role to make better use of your strengths, or switch to a more strengths-friendly career track.

YOU DON'T HAVE TO SWIM UPSTREAM

As a first-time director with HP, Sandy Lieske found herself working on a program that was highly technically complex. Despite always having relied on her strong technical skills, she felt thwarted. "I didn't understand why things were so hard and why I felt so badly all the time," Sandy says.

What happened next had a profound impact on her approach to leadership. A project manager on Sandy's team took her aside and pointed out that the difficulty she was experiencing was not about the technology. Her challenges were managing change and aligning the group behind a clear vision of where it needed to go.

"This required a focus on influencing, which was not one of my top strengths," admitted Sandy. She enlisted a consultant to help her articulate a comprehensive vision for the program. Then Sandy partnered with a change-management expert to help garner executives' support. That vision became a rallying cry for the entire organization and the basis for a multiyear strategic roadmap. "The results were amazing," says Sandy. The program was expected to cause signification attrition, but only one person left. Sandy went on to become a research and development executive with HP, and she now lectures in engineering management at a research-focused public university.

Sandy became a passionate advocate for and practitioner of a strengths-based approach to leadership, where you exploit your strengths, get help when you need it, and build a team of people with complementary strengths. It's fueled her own development and that of countless others she has mentored. "Don't swim upstream," says Sandy. "When you internalize your strengths, it allows you to make the right career choices to position you to operate at your best every day." She recommends these steps to identify your strengths:

- **Identify your career-defining successes.** Think about roles or situations in which you've done your absolute best, when you've been the most energized. "Look back at the times you've most enjoyed your work and when you feel you've made the biggest contribution," Sandy says. Identify assignments that capitalized on your strengths.
- **Don't fixate on fixing weaknesses.** Focusing on your weaknesses can be stressful and demoralizing, and it can deplete your confidence and self-esteem.[7] Reframing how most of us would view weaknesses, Sandy says that it's important to understand what your "bottom strengths" are, but you should not spend all your time trying to improve them. Candidly admitting that people skills are not among her top strengths, Sandy says, "Empathy is one of my bottom strengths, but someone on my staff had empathy in their top five."
- **Don't swim upstream.** If you're in a job that doesn't capitalize on your strengths, look for opportunities that do. Summon up the courage to talk with your manager about augmenting your role or sculpting it into something that aligns more closely with what you do best.
- **Dare to declare your deficits.** Once you move beyond the discomfort of what you don't do well, you can become quite pragmatic. Look for people whose skills round out your deficits. Coming from that mindset, obstacles like Sandy's challenging

project become opportunities to collaborate with others who have complementary strengths. End result: Everyone gets to shine.

WHO ARE YOU, REALLY?

At the beginning of this chapter, I promised we would focus on answering the question, "Who am I as a leader, really?" To help do this, we're going to break your strengths down into three categories:

- Professional strengths
- Leadership strengths
- Character strengths

This process will help you better understand what you bring to the table as a leader that's truly unique.

If you have a tough time making an objective self-assessment for any of these areas, outsource it. This is an opportunity to practice opening yourself up to honest critique. Ask others, such as your manager, mentor, and friends at work. Feedback, if you're willing to hear it and even if it stings at first, can be one of the most powerful engines behind your development as a leader.

> Feedback, if you're willing to hear it and even if it stings at first, can be one of the most powerful engines behind your development as a leader.

RECOGNIZE YOUR PROFESSIONAL STRENGTHS

Start by looking at your professional strengths—skills, talents, or domain expertise you've developed in your industry or profession.

Setting modesty aside, reflect on your career-defining successes and the professional skills and expertise that made them possible. Think about what you're working on when people go out of their way to praise you or thank you for work you've done well. You might shrug and say, "It's nothing," and it might seem like it, but *that's the point*. Others were wowed by your work, and it came effortlessly to you.

OWN IT

What Are Your Professional Strengths?

If you're not familiar with your professional strengths, or you haven't reflected on them in a while, here are some questions to ask yourself that will help you get to know them and capitalize on them. Pick three or more to answer:

- What are you are really good at?
- Are there skills or talents you've been downplaying or apologizing for?
- What have you learned about yourself from collaborating with others whose strengths differ from but complement your own?
- Which strengths would you like to further develop?
- What were you doing when work felt hard, stressful, or demoralizing?
- What are your "bottom strengths" (aka weaknesses)?
- What work would you pay someone not to have to do?

Jot down your answers. When you're done, tuck the list away somewhere you won't easily forget. You'll draw on it later in this chapter to lock focus on some core capabilities at which you dazzle and shine.

For now, dream up one action you can take in coming days that uses a professional strength. When you approach that task, go all in. Immerse yourself in it and let your greatness glow. But that's not all. I also want you to diplomatically deflect one task related to an "unstrength"—a task that feels like a grind and dulls your shine.

OUTSOURCE IT

What Are Your Professional Strengths?

Approach three people who know your work well enough to offer insight into your strengths. Here are some questions to ask:

- What am I good at?
- Which of my skills or talents are uniquely valuable to the work I am doing?
- Which strengths should I focus on and continue to develop?
- What kinds of work should I steer away from?

Assessment tools like the DISC Index, CliftonStrengths, and Hogan Assessments provide objective, external perspectives on your natural strengths and work style. If you've taken any in the past, now's an ideal time to refamiliarize yourself with the results.

REVEAL YOUR LEADERSHIP STRENGTHS

In Chapter 1, you began to pay attention to your leadership catnip moments and identified whether you're a change, people, results, service, or thought leader. Now it's time to get more granular and identify a signature leadership style that's entirely your own.

"What are your leadership strengths?" That's a question I ask in a survey that participants complete before attending my intensive, daylong *Poised for Leadership* workshop, which helps emerging leaders create a roadmap to break into management or technical leadership positions. Most attendees aren't quite in management or technical leadership roles (though they aspire to be).

As I prepare for a workshop, one of my favorite activities is to read each group's responses and compile a list of the attendees' self-reported strengths on a slide titled "A leader is someone who . . . "

I've found that their collective response paints a remarkably inspiring and detailed picture of leadership at its best. On workshop day, I read them the list titled "This is what being a leader means to you."

Below is a list of 50 qualities of a leader, crowdsourced from 1,200 workshop respondents, that we'll use later to define *your* signature leadership strengths. But first, simply skim the list:

50 Leadership Qualities

A leader is someone who:

1. Sees the big picture
2. Thinks strategically
3. Sets the vision and direction
4. Displays a strong business acumen
5. Strives for continuous improvement
6. Possesses strong interpersonal skills
7. Communicates with transparency
8. Delivers effective speaking presentations
9. Gives open, honest, and direct feedback
10. Listens to understand
11. Asks the right questions at the right time
12. Manages crises and conflict with ease
13. Finds middle ground and a path forward
14. Drives results
15. Embraces and leads change
16. Acts decisively
17. Stays goal oriented and solution focused
18. Strives to accomplish what she commits to doing
19. Takes ownership
20. Sets high standards
21. Takes risks
22. Wins trust and earns respect
23. Operates with integrity and fairness
24. Has a thirst for learning
25. Shares know-how
26. Shows empathy
27. Leads by example
28. Stands up for what she believes in
29. Inspires and empowers others
30. Influences without authority
31. Manages up, down, and across
32. Builds teams and fosters teamwork
33. Rallies people to achieve a common goal or purpose

34. Delegates
35. Sets clear expectations
36. Trusts others to do their jobs without micromanaging
37. Enables others to be successful
38. Removes obstacles from a team's path
39. Gives positive and constructive feedback
40. Allows people to learn from mistakes
41. Mentors, coaches, and develops people
42. Provides people with the tools and autonomy to get things done
43. Acts as a strong advocate for those she manages and mentors
44. Gives credit where it is due
45. Celebrates others' achievements
46. Rewards good performance
47. Understands the motivations of others to inspire them in their work
48. Identifies and utilizes others' strengths
49. Cares about the well-being of the team
50. Helps others shine

You can download a printable, sharable list of 100 leadership qualities at www.jomiller.com/100qualities.

OWN IT

What Are Your Leadership Strengths?

To prep for this exercise, go back to your notes from Chapter 1 and reread the list of your personal acts of leadership —your leadership catnip. No matter how small or simple, these actions are evidence of your natural leadership strengths. Also take a moment now to think about your leadership type—change, people, results, service, or thought leader. Think back to what you learned about yourself from those activities.

Now, take things a little slower, and go through the list of 50 leadership qualities with more of a strategic mindset:

- Return to the list of "50 Leadership Qualities," and highlight all of the qualities you already see in yourself and any you'd like to improve on.

- Next, narrow that entire list down to the 10 qualities that best represent how you'd like to lead. Remember to focus on your strengths and innate leadership style.
- Now it's time to narrow that list down even more. From your list of 10, pick the 3 qualities that best represent the leadership strengths you'd most like to own and be known for 12 months from today. You can partly achieve this by grouping similar qualities into one category such as "Sees the big picture" and "Sets the vision and direction." In your group of 3, try to include two that you're already strong in and one that's more aspirational—an attribute you're still growing into, but that you feel predisposed to become great at.

Here are some results that workshop participants walked away with when doing this exercise:

- *Medical safety officer:* Sees the big picture. Trusts others to do their jobs without micromanaging. Inspires and empowers others.
- *Manager for quality and system performance:* Identifies and utilizes others' strengths. Builds teams and fosters teamwork. Understands the motivations of others to inspire them in their work.
- *Engineering program manager:* Listens to understand. Possesses strong interpersonal skills. Communicates with transparency.

Put your three leadership strengths somewhere where you'll see the words every day as a reminder to play up these qualities and own the heck out of them. Write them on a sticky note, take a pic and save it as the home screen on your phone, or set a daily popup reminder in your calendar. In Chapter 6, we'll cover using your strengths to commit bold, unforgettable acts of leadership, but for now, the goal is committing small, everyday acts that align with those leadership qualities.

OUTSOURCE IT

What Are Your Leadership Strengths?

Show the long list of 100 leadership qualities at www.jomiller
.com/100qualities to a few people who know you well and ask them
to identify 3 qualities they associate with you. Ask: "Which of these
qualities best describe my leadership strengths?"

CELEBRATE YOUR CHARACTER STRENGTHS

Listen up, because here's where it all gets interesting.

There's a correlation between job satisfaction and having a signature strength of character—such as infectious enthusiasm, empathy, firmness, or feistiness—that's *less typical* among those in your occupation.[8] Think of this as the way your personal values and disposition show up in your everyday actions—and make you stand out. If you want greater gratification from your work, go beyond discovering your professional strengths and *what* you do and look at *how* you do what you do. Identify your uncommon strengths of character: those quirky, individualistic traits that make you stand out.

One of Tracy Joshua's strengths of character is courage. Tracy, a vice president of indirect procurement with a Fortune 500 company in the food industry, learned to use her courage muscle at an early age. In elementary school, Tracy's friend Cynthia was constantly being picked on by a girl named Shirley, who was tall for their grade. One day, Tracy saw Shirley bullying Cynthia and decided that she had had enough. "I stood tall, looked Shirley in the eye, and said 'You will not hurt my friend,'" says Tracy. Almost immediately, Shirley stopped and apologized.

In standing up for someone else, Tracy brought to light her gift: using her voice to speak up for others. Tracy also credits her extended family who instilled the importance of being bold in the face of adversity, and this transferred to her professional life.

There may be other talented leaders at multinational food companies who are responsible for procuring $3 billion in goods and services, but there is only one who brings such fierce determination to stand up for others in the way that Tracy does. She is often one of the few women—and in most cases, the only woman of color—in the room. "When you are the only one or one of a few, it is even more critical for you to speak up for those who do not have a voice," says Tracy.

Tracy encourages others to be courageously authentic, letting their strengths of character shine. She says, "When you have the courage to use your character, intellect, feelings, and soul, coupled with your power and influence, you can help make humankind better." Everybody's thumbprint is different, so get comfortable in your skin, and focus on your strengths. You are the only one who gets to define who you are. "Walk in your own personal greatness with confidence," says Tracy.

You're much more than a rock star engineer, project manager, biologist, or HR business partner. You have unique character strengths that you can't help but infuse into your work. These are informed by your core beliefs and values, successes, struggles, failures, personal theme song, and even spirit animal, if that's your thing. It's not just what you do. It's how you do it.

> **Everybody's thumbprint is different, so get comfortable in your skin and focus on your strengths.**

If you're not certain what your character strengths are, this is an easy one to crowdsource. That's what Liza, a field sales manager in one of my group coaching programs, did. Liza sent text messages to six colleagues, asking "What three character traits would you say best describe me?" Within minutes she had begun to receive feedback, and the answers were a revelation. As a result, Liza made a small but meaningful course correction in her career path to make the most of her character strengths.

In the next exercise, you'll identify a couple of your top character strengths—that is, those signature traits that differentiate you from others in your profession.

OWN IT

What Are Your Character Strengths?

Write down your answer to this question: What are your top three character strengths that are *less typical* among your peers?

OUTSOURCE IT

What Are Your Character Strengths?

Send text messages to six people, asking "What three character traits would you say best describe me?" You can ask your mentors, manager, and colleagues, but in this instance, they don't all need to be people from your work life. Family members, friends, life partners, neighbors, or members of a community have seen your spirit glow and can help here too.

MAKE SELF-EVALUATION YOUR COMPASS

If you're a new or aspiring leader, it may be tempting to emulate successful leaders or adopt a leadership style that's prevalent within your organization. Not so fast, says Karen Stuckey, a senior vice president of private brand procurement for Walmart.

Here is one of the lessons Karen would tell to her early-leader self: "When we're new in our leadership journey, we tend to rely on assessment tools or other people's feedback to help us know what to do." Instead, she would encourage you to use the feedback you receive to develop a strong internal compass for insightful and accurate self-evaluation. "The best gift you can give yourself is to focus on doing a clear self-assessment," she says. When you put a priority on understanding yourself and your innate leadership strengths—and you bring your natural, authentic self to whatever role you're playing—you will be more effective, regardless of your style.

WHAT ARE YOUR STANDOUT STRENGTHS?

When all's said and done, the lists of your professional, leadership, and character strengths you've been creating are *your* lists. Their ultimate purpose is to support and empower you to fully embrace your existing strengths, while gently nudging you to step up to the vision of yourself as the leader you're striving to become.

So while incorporating feedback from others is critical to the process, you're the ultimate authority—the final arbiter of what your strengths are. Internalize them and you'll feel more focused, unencumbered, and authentic as you go about your work.

OWN IT

What Are Your Standout Strengths?

Thanks to the work you've done throughout this chapter, you're now surrounded by lists. Lists of *professional strengths*, *leadership strengths*, and *character strengths*. If they seem overwhelming, don't worry, it's by design.

For this exercise, I want you to gather up those three lists of answers and compile them all into one long, rambling, gratifying list.

Now, take a moment to read through those attributes and let it all sink in. This is a giant mashup of everything you're great at. It's what's unique to you—and it has currency. Hit "cancel" on swimming upstream. Any future career-related decisions you make should incorporate and honor these qualities.

And, for the very last step in this process, review your list and highlight a small handful of your most formidable, standout strengths. What does your gut tell you that you could become world class at, if you really set your mind to it? Write down your standout strengths, and keep the list close at hand as you move on to Chapter 3, where you'll use them to pinpoint an influential leadership niche.

OUTSOURCE IT

What Are Your Standout Strengths?

This one's not for the faint of heart, so choose someone like your mentor or work best friend who not only has opinions about what you're great at but also isn't afraid to tell them to you straight.

Share your list of professional, leadership, and character strengths with her, and ask, "Which of these are my standout strengths?"

DREAM BIGGER

There's one more question to consider before exiting Chapter 2, and it's a big one: Are you aiming high enough?

Pamela Stewart's experience with audacious goal setting predates her professional career. Today, as senior vice president of national retail sales at the Coca-Cola Company, Pamela is a seasoned "goal-getter." But when she entered high school, her mom had just gotten a divorce, and the family's finances were tight. At that time, no one in Pamela's family had ever attended college, and there were few African American female leaders as role models in her life.

"I didn't have a mentor whom I could call up, so I defined and envisioned who I wanted to be," says Pamela. While her peers aspired to be doctors or lawyers, she wanted to become the US secretary of state or a United Nations ambassador. As Pamela mapped out her plan, she realized it would require a full-ride college scholarship.

The next four school years required a lot of hard work, including applying herself academically, participating in extracurricular activities, and excelling in sports. But it paid off because Pamela entered college on a full scholarship, becoming a first-generation scholar.

"I would encourage you not to define your boldest dreams by your history. Dream bigger," says Pamela. She presses mentees to expand their vision of who they can become, saying, "If you feel 50 percent or more confident that you can achieve the dream, you're not dreaming big enough. Make sure that it is truly bold and aspirational."

When your job becomes second nature, or you're too enamored by the credibility and respect that you have in your role, it's time to think about taking new risks, Pamela says. "If you wake up every day knowing what to expect, and you've learned all that there is to learn in your role, that's the moment to step out of complacency."

Now that you've connected with your unique capabilities—your standout strengths—imagine where they might take you. Is it time to recalibrate your aspirations, dream bigger, and set an even loftier goal?

When I ask workshop attendees to name their most important career goal, the answers, unsurprisingly, are incredibly diverse. Here are some examples, in case you're in need of some inspiration:

> **Is it time to recalibrate your aspirations, dream bigger, and set an even loftier goal?**

- Become a trusted partner to my company's executives
- Invent new technologies and be recognized as a major contributor at my organization
- Work in a job where I can see the results of my work have an effect on people
- Keep learning new things and keep my brand and reputation in high gear
- Develop in-depth expertise in areas I own
- Become a senior vice president
- Find a role where I can really shine
- Lead a major strategic initiative
- Move to a role where my big-picture and communication strengths are valued
- Step out of the shadows to manage a bigger group
- Lead a department while maintaining my work-life balance
- Manage a separate profit and loss (P&L)
- Put a customer experience strategy in place for the business
- Get at least one promotion

The next exercise asks you to dream bigger and declare where you'd like to be in three years, by setting a lofty career or leadership goal.

OWN IT

What's Your Lofty Goal?

Where do you imagine yourself being in three years?

Review the questions below and choose one that calls to you the loudest. Then, start freewriting for at least one page, and give yourself the time and space to dream up your answer:

- What's your highest vision or aspiration for your professional self?
- What outcome would be the most tangible expression of your professional purpose?
- What contributions would you find most meaningful?
- What accomplishment would be deeply satisfying?

What's your lofty, bold-ass, brassy, electrifying, vertigo-inducing goal? Put pen to paper or fingertips to keyboard and name it. Then, commit to it and make it your mission.

CHAPTER 2 WRAP-UP

Your strengths are your natural competitive advantage. Identifying, embracing, employing, and amplifying your strengths can form the foundation of an extraordinary career. When *you do you*, it sets you apart.

Now that you've worked through the exercises in Chapters 1 and 2, you're surrounded by lists that include your professional, leadership, and character strengths, plus a summary of your standout strengths. You've dreamed bigger, and you've committed to going after a lofty, audacious career goal.

The next step is to zoom into these strengths and figure out how you can use them to ignite your passions and fill a gap within your organization. That's what Chapter 3 is all about. You will walk away with a clear understanding of your leadership niche so you can sculpt a role—or even better, a career trajectory—around your authenticity, uniqueness, and strengths. Let's keep moving!

What's Your Superpower?

Claim Your Leadership Niche

> *You have one lifetime to live.*
> *Choose gigs that feed your soul.*
> **—Sara Sperling,**
> partner, Oxegen Consulting

We're all familiar with the adage: "Do what you love." While I too want you to love what you do, let's be real: there are also bills to pay.

In the previous chapters, you paid attention to the acts of leadership that come easily to you. You learned about the five types of leaders and the one you most strongly identify with. You investigated your professional, leadership, and character strengths, and you highlighted your standout strengths.

Now, the trick is to find the sweet spot where your strengths align with your passions and an organizational need. I call this your *leadership niche*. Defining yours is the most important exercise in this book, and this chapter will help you figure out precisely how to do that. Once you know your leadership niche, you can claim it and develop the heck out of it. It will become your career superpower, your professional awesome-sauce. Construct a career from within your niche and you'll be flat-out sought after.

If you've ever been in your niche, you'll know how rewarding it is. You come to work every day to do those things you truly enjoy and that utilize your greatest strengths, all while delivering a much-needed service. It's gratifying. You feel valued. You'll know when you've identified your own niche because discovering it feels like a mini-epiphany (a former colleagues calls this an "epiphanette."). You feel energized and ready to move forward, without delay.

Here's another way to look at it. Before setting out to climb a ladder, it pays to take a step back and confirm: "Is my ladder propped against the right building?" That momentary pause might just position you to climb to heights that are scarcely imaginable.

WE ALL HAVE AN OPPORTUNITY
TO BE INFLUENCERS

A few years ago, Liz Brenner, a former vice president of human resources, was feeling uninspired. After spending five years in her company's technology marketing team, it felt like a grind. Liz says, "It was really getting to me." So she set aside some time to reflect on the things that she cared about and what got her out of bed in the morning.

As Liz thought back to the times when she had felt most engaged in her work, the values of diversity, inclusion, and leadership kept coming to mind and clamoring for attention. From there, she did some reconnaissance inside her company, including networking and trying to uncover projects and programs that might allow her to tap into these interests. Liz volunteered for her company's Business Women's Network as a way of testing out her hunches and getting closer to the work that intrigued her. "It brought passion, excitement, and satisfaction back to my professional life," she says. "I didn't know it at the time, but I was creating my own brand."

Liz made a pivot, leaving behind her role as a senior director of global marketing. She melded her marketing background and passion for talent development, landing in a new discipline at the intersection of marketing and human resources: talent marketing. In that role, Liz thrived, eventually being promoted to SAP's vice president of human resources marketing and engagement. She led initiatives that borrowed from marketing strategies, putting employees at the center of HR strategy, because, like customers, they are central to a company's success.

"Seek out opportunities and roles that match up with your passions, so you can bring your best self to work," says Liz. "We all have an opportunity to be influencers in our area of expertise," she adds. "The best thing you can do for yourself is to invest some time in figuring out who you are and what your niche is."

BE FAMOUS FOR SOMETHING

What's the best game plan for career security and mitigating risks? Is it:

- A. Becoming a good all-rounder
- B. Broadly diversifying your portfolio of skills
- C. Investing in a wide range of strengths to hedge against volatility in the job market

Sorry. I set you up with a trick question. The answer is "none of the above."

You are *not* a mutual fund, my friend. Diversification will fatten up your retirement account but undernourish your career.

"Be famous for something, and know your claim to fame," says one executive I interviewed. She advises newer leaders to stay narrowly focused on doing work where they can most add value and make an impact.

Now, you might be thinking, "Be famous for something. But what?" The answer to that question is where you'll find your leadership niche. It's where your strengths and passions align with an organizational need. This is the thing you're most likely to become memorable, noted, recognized, or renowned for.

MISSTEP 3

Being good at a lot of things and famous for none of them is career Misstep 3.

The alternative Leaderly Move is *claiming a niche that aligns your strengths and passions with your value to your organization*.

When you own a uniquely valuable leadership niche, benefits include the following:

- Career decisions or dilemmas you may have struggled with become less daunting, easier to resolve, or even instantly solved.

- You understand which roles to aggressively pursue because they're a great fit for you and which ones to diplomatically say no to.

- You understand what additional skills to build or qualifications to pursue, and even whom to seek out as your mentors and advocates.

- You can differentiate yourself, even in a highly competitive team.

- You can build wildly successful collaborations with rock star colleagues whose strengths complement yours.

BE A ROCK STAR

There are tangible benefits to owning a standout niche. Liz Harr, partner at marketing consultancy Hinge, studied the career trajectories of 130 brightly shining industry stars—"Visible Experts™"—in professional services, and their customers. "For starters, their earnings are higher," says Liz.

The study Liz coauthored identified the levels experts progress through as they become increasingly visible. Which of these levels describes you today, and which would you like to attain?

- **Resident experts** are people who are respected and valued within their firm but relatively unknown outside it—and they command a fee more than twice that of the average professional.

- **Rising industry stars** have found their niche and frequently speak and write about it. They can command almost four times the average fee, and (and some could argue that this is even more valuable) they can be choosier about the work they accept.

- **Industry rock stars** have carved out a niche of national renown. They attract a wealth of opportunities, and they no longer need to hustle for work, media mentions, or speaking engagements.

Instead, they spend time filtering and prioritizing what to work on. Let this sink in: the market is willing to fork out over seven times more for a professional services industry rock star than an average professional.

- And don't even get me started on what **global superstars** can command. (It's 13 times that of an average professional.*)[1]

I know you're not in this only for the money, so consider these escalating fee levels as a proxy for how your value, reach, and difference-making ability can multiply as you become increasingly well known.

With all the attention these stars attract, do they cause others to miss out? Are they hogging the limited space in the spotlight? Not at all, explains Liz. In fact, it's the opposite. Industry stars confer a strong halo effect on their companies and colleagues. Think about it: when you meet someone whose expertise you're wowed by, you're likely to believe the company they keep is rarified too. As stars rise, they illuminate others.

Now, here's the kicker. The vast majority of industry stars interviewed insisted they are no smarter or luckier than their peers. Instead, they were gutsy and determined. Says Liz, "They found their niche and refused to give up until they stood out." That busts the myths that you must start out as a good all-rounder and fit in before you stand out. Liz says, "Specialization allows you to forge ahead without the noise that generalized knowledge brings to the table."

There's value in being visible.

You can step into the spotlight without eclipsing others.

You don't have to be brilliant or lucky to stake your claim to professional fame.

You just need to be focused and feisty.

> **You don't have to be brilliant or lucky to stake your claim to professional fame.**

---

* Curiously, the market demand for a global superstar is one-fourth of that of a nationally known rock star. Achieving the height of fame has a price. Adjust your aspirations accordingly.

HARNESS YOUR SUPERPOWERS

While interviewing C-level women leaders for her book *Pushback: How Smart Women Ask—and Stand Up—for What They Want,* leadership author and speaker Selena Rezvani, the vice president of consulting and research at Be Leaderly, had a revelation that left her flat-out amazed. Almost every woman Selena interviewed noted that she didn't hammer herself for her weaknesses, but actively, strategically cultivated her gifts so she could call on them in any situation. You must do the same. Says Selena, "Harness your superpowers and capitalize on them to benefit your career."

You're no different than Tina, the whip-smart corporate finance analyst in the Introduction who transformed herself from a self-described pooper-scooper into her team's change agent, or Liz Brenner, uninspired tech marketer who pivoted into an engaged talent leader. You're no less capable of redefining yourself. You have what it takes to carve out a unique, valuable, even transformational leadership niche.

Identifying your niche begins with giving up the allure of becoming good at many things but famous for none of them.

If this sounds risky, consider the alternative: if you try to define yourself too broadly and try to be all things to all people, you'll miss out on opportunities to provide anything meaningful to anyone. The more narrowly you define your focus, the more likely it is that you can own your chosen professional space and become widely known among those who value what you have to offer.

You are so much more than your job history, title, responsibilities, and even your highly visible accomplishments. It's not enough to get As in school or think that because you're smart or get things done, everyone will see that, observes Amy Radin. Amy has held roles as chief marketing officer or chief innovation officer with top brands including Citi, E*TRADE, and AXA. "The more you specialize, the more easily people will understand what the heck you do. It's not about narrowness. It's about claiming your specialty," she explains. Much like Irish author and poet Orna Ross pointed out, you can have anything you want; you just can't have everything you want.

In claiming your specialty, you can demonstrate substance that goes far beyond the sum of such parts as your education, accomplishments, and work history. But how should you decide what your focus should be?

Let's break it down, element by element.

THREE ESSENTIAL ELEMENTS OF YOUR LEADERSHIP NICHE

Listen up, because this part's important.

Seasoned leaders like Liz Brenner are able to succinctly and effortlessly articulate what they do well. They know their leadership niche. Most of the people you admire, whether they're your professional role models, sought-after experts, celebrities, or famous athletes, have claimed their niche and capitalized on it. It is why they are where they are today. Not everyone stumbles effortlessly into their niche. I came across mine almost by accident after years of trial and error. Some people discover theirs through deliberate reflection or opening themselves up to feedback, and you can too.

Ready to uncover your superpower, your personal awesome-sauce, your leadership niche? This will take some work, but it is very much worth the effort. Let's set up the base for what we'll achieve by the end of this chapter.

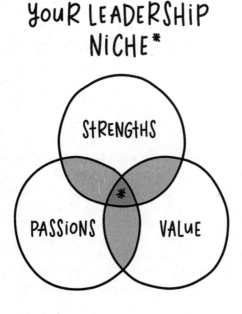

Grab a piece of paper and draw yourself a Venn diagram with three overlapping circles. You can also download the worksheet at www .jomiller.com/niche. The three circles will represent three essential, foundational elements that harmonize to form your leadership niche, or superpower. This niche is the key to discovering the work that has you sit up and say, "*This* is what I was built for":

Circle 1. What are your strengths?

Circle 2. What are your passions?

Circle 3. What does your organization value?*

WHAT ARE YOUR STRENGTHS?

In Chapter 2 you comprehensively documented your professional, leadership, and character strengths and narrowed them down to your standout strengths—those you'd most love to be sought out for. In this chapter, you'll connect the dots from these top strengths to the work you love to do that is also a valuable asset to your organization.

Now let's dive in for deeper exploration of the other two essential elements: your passions and value to your organization.

WHAT ARE YOUR PASSIONS?

When determining your leadership niche, the next element to consider consists of your passions: those activities or areas of expertise that you can't help but feel fired up about.

---

* You might be familiar with this as Jim Collins's Hedgehog Concept from his book *Good to Great: Why Some Companies Make the Leap and Others Don't* (New York: Harper Collins, 2001), named for philosopher Isaiah Berlin's interpretation of an ancient Greek parable: "The fox knows many things, but the hedgehog knows one big thing." (1) What you are deeply passionate about? (2) What can you be the best in the world at? And (3) What best drives your economic or resource engine? https://www .jimcollins.com/concepts/the-hedgehog-concept.html.

Or you may have come across the widely riffed on career sweet spot model, which combines what you love doing, what you're good at, and what pays you well.

Women at my leadership workshops often say they're tired of settling for work that is making them feel detached or dispirited. They're often frustrated because they want challenges that spark their passion. "I am still trying to figure out what I want to be when I grow up," said one. Here's what others had to say. See if you can relate to any of these statements:

- I want to do work I'm passionate about where I can have an impact at work every day.
- I would like to add value to the company and organization and see the results of my work affect people.
- I have little passion for my day-to-day work. I feel like I am not utilized well.
- I'd like to find an area I am interested in and excel at it.
- I would like to continue to grow and move into an area that aligns with my passion.
- I want to learn what I can do that uses my strengths and that will have an impact on the company and others, and yet I want to love what I am doing.

Among the more established leaders I interviewed, one obvious constant I noticed was the enjoyment and enthusiasm they had for their work. Here's how three of them connected with work that they find fascinating and fulfilling.

Choose Gigs That Feed Your Soul

When I spoke to Sara Sperling, a partner at Oxegen Consulting, her character strength of infectious enthusiasm quickly became evident, and it was not long before her philosophy for making career decisions did too.

As a math major in college, Sara was told that she had two career options: teacher or actuary. "But that didn't feed my soul," says Sara. "So instead, I kept choosing jobs that did." Sara worked in academia and for a women's professional soccer league before finding her way into high tech—and eventually a role that she never could have predicted.

At the time of our interview, Sara was working at Facebook where she had started out onboarding new hires and creating an engineering leadership program. But she was also looking for her community. Upon discovering that the company didn't have formal employee resource groups (ERGs), she helped reinvigorate an informal group now known as Pride@Facebook. Word got around, and executives with all kinds of diversity-related questions started coming to her for help, as did employees who wanted to form their own ERGs. "Mind you," says Sara, "this wasn't part of my job. It was just something I did on the side that I was passionate about."

Eventually, Facebook's leadership caught on and saw that there was real value to having someone focus on diversity and inclusion. They asked Sara to start and lead the company's diversity and inclusion function.

"One of the things that I've been passionate about throughout my life is being there for lesbian, gay, bisexual, and transgender (LGBT) youth— letting them know that they're not alone and that there is a lot of support for them in the LGBT community," she shares. Sara was able to make a direct link from that cause to building an inclusive corporate culture, where employees are more likely to feel like they can be themselves. "If they can do that, then they're going to do amazing work."

Still, Sara took a couple of weeks to think before accepting the role. "I had no background in this. I didn't go to school for it. I had never even been to a diversity conference," she says. All she had was raw enthusiasm, but her leadership trusted that she could do it and do it well. Sara took a leap of faith.

Not only was it a way to make an impact on people inside of the company but, with over a billion Facebook users, it was also an opportunity to make an even larger impact in the world. Sara helped the company create its Transgender & Gender Identity Policy. And her leap of faith landed her on the cover of *Diversity Executive* magazine and on *Business Insider*'s lists of "13 Secret Rock Stars of Silicon Valley" and "31 Most Important LGBT People in Tech."

If you take a job for the money or the title, that gratification will be relatively short-lived, compared to a role doing work that you sincerely love, explains Sara. So what are Sara's top criteria for assessing new career opportunities? It's an impressively short list. "I ask 'Am I going to be excited to walk in the door every day?' and 'Can I make an impact on somebody?' That's it!" Sara says.

Sara encourages others to gravitate toward work they're infectiously enthusiastic about too. "I really think people want to wake up every day excited about where they're going to go for most of the day," she says.

Break Free from Being Boxed In

The most accomplished leaders I've worked with have a common trait: they are acutely aware of what drains them and what sustains them. They're biased toward doing work that engages and energizes them, and they're protective of where they invest their most precious resource: their time.

After 11 years in financial services, Allison Unkraut took a courageous leap. Allison was a vice president in an industry she was comfortable with, but she didn't feel like she was in the right role within the right industry, so she decided to make a complete career change and move into an entry-level role.

Allison was working in product management with a bank when she and her team began to look for ways to expand relationships with their top 100 business banking customers, segmenting them into groups as a way to offer more personalized attention. "It sparked my passion for understanding our customers more," says Allison. "I got super excited." Then the bank was acquired. The new owner acknowledged that this customer-centric focus was a great idea but declined to pursue it further. Allison was disappointed. "I realized I could be making a larger impact outside of financial services."

With a mix of fear and excitement, Allison made her move, joining a consumer data insights company in the retail and grocery industry. She left the relative stability of financial services and a role managing a large team to become an individual contributor with a small, unproven company in an industry she had no experience in. "I went from being the go-to-person to the one who knew nothing," says Allison.

"My manager was amazing and took the time to coach and train me," says Allison, who peppered her manager with questions and frantically took notes in meetings. She leaned heavily on her top strengths of collaboration and communication during that time, and she made sure to always contribute even as she was learning. She amplified her strengths, and she was clear and up front about what she didn't know.

That's not to say that she never experienced doubts. Three months in, Allison felt sure she'd made a big mistake, and she called an old boss at the bank to ask if he would hire her back. "Absolutely not," he replied. "You need to do exactly what you're doing now." This confirmed exactly what Allison needed to hear and strengthened her resolve to stay put. She says, "I am still thankful to him for saying no to me that day. Now I am in a job I absolutely love in an industry that's changing dramatically. I love the pace of change." Every day brings something new.

In the 13 years following her career reboot, Allison worked her way up through a variety of roles, and she now leads 150 merchandising employees as 84.51°'s senior vice president of customer strategy and activation, working with Kroger to enhance customers' shopping experiences. She was recently named one of *Progressive Grocer*'s "Top Women in Grocery." "It's been a great journey," she says. "I have had an opportunity to learn more and contribute more," proving that sometimes you have to slow down in order to speed up.

At times, we drift away from work that feels meaningful and provides a sense of purpose and fulfillment. We can get typecast and boxed into roles or career paths that are a mismatch for our passions. So it's a good practice to periodically pause to reassess your path and readjust if necessary, especially if work leaves you feeling depleted or defeated.

Allison's successful path is evidence that it's possible to take a step back, make a bold, courageous move, and course correct. "Have the courage to be true to who you are, but also be willing to grow in ways that will let you continue to advance," she says. You can be exactly who you are and still be a leader. "If you spend your time trying to be someone that you think other people want you to be, you will exhaust yourself. You just won't be successful."

Prioritize What Fuels You

By paying attention to what energizes you and fuels you professionally, you can seize opportunities to prioritize the work that's most fulfilling.

Looking back, my first attempt at a career was like a business suit that looked incredible on the hanger but was ill fitting as hell once I tried it on. I exchanged it for one that was a more comfortable fit, and then I hit a new challenge.

I had left my job at the boutique staffing agency and started a little business as a trainer and coach. I enjoyed the work, and my business was doing OK, but I had noticed that the coaches who were *really* thriving were the ones who'd developed a specialty such as executive, wealth, or spiritual energy coaching. None of those options grabbed me, so I hired a coach of my own, named Megan. I told her that our goal was to find my niche. One of my first homework assignments from Megan was to write an excruciatingly long list of areas I could specialize in. There were 50, to be precise. I wasn't sure if I should be coaching staffing agents, HR managers, or high-tech sales people, but I added those and more to my list.

Megan and I were reviewing the list, which she'd helped me whittle down to five possibilities, when she said, "Jo, when you talk about coaching women in leadership, you sound 10 times more excited than everything else." I left our coaching session and wrote "women's leadership coach" in my email signature with a clarity of purpose that's rarely wavered since.

Many years later, I'm still insatiably curious about how women around the world advance into positions of leadership and influence—especially in male-dominated industries. I have an inner drive to deliver programs where I can see women get excited about stepping into the leadership pipeline, and I have enlisted others to help bring about a future with more women in positions of corporate leadership.

"Prioritize that which fuels you," says Katherine Durham, former chief marketing officer and vice president of individual disability insurance with The Standard. "Pay attention to the peak moments in your career," she says. "You were probably working harder than ever, putting in a lot of hours, but having a blast. Identify what was going on in those moments."

Katherine points out that we typically don't give ourselves the gift of time for this type of deep reflection. It may take writing it out or thinking about it while you're exercising or getting feedback from someone who knows you well. Or you may need to verbally process it by talking it out with someone. Dedicate some time to reflecting on this.

Don't Discover Your Passion

Passion drives performance, and this matters—a lot. When a team at Deloitte examined what makes work not feel like work, they discovered a startling divide: 87 percent of America's workforce are contributing less than their full potential because they lack passion for what they do.[2] The rare individuals who have connected their passion to their profession—for example, Liz Brenner, Sara Sperling, and Allison Unkraut—outearn, outlearn, and outperform their peers. They also have the fierce resilience it takes to conquer the inevitable challenges, setbacks, and disruptions that pepper our modern workplaces.

Despite what your Instagram feed might lead you to believe, the notion that you can just go discover your life's calling and in doing so unleash your passion is a bit misguided. The reality is more nuanced and worth taking time to understand.

The idea that we all have a grand, enduring, preprogrammed passion for a fixed area of interest has been debunked by researchers at Yale and Stanford.[3] Rather than going all-in to *discover* one, deep, intrinsic passion that can provide you with an endless source of motivation, they found it's possible to actually *develop* passion for something you enjoy doing.

You don't have to wait to *discover* passion.

You can dive right in and *develop* it.

Developing a passion is something you work at, persist with, and grow into.

Here's another plot twist: we're not all that effective at predicting where our passions lie, and we are more likely to stumble across them, the way Sara Sperling did. If you have identified your professional passions and can apply them in your work, congratulations. You're one of 13 percent who have.

> Developing a passion is something you work at, persist with, and grow into.

But if you're less clear, remember "Find your passion" is vague advice that's mildly helpful at best. Here's a more specific path. Find something you enjoy and *develop* a passion for it. Or choose some areas to dabble in and explore to make it easier for passion to find you. Explore an interest. Try stuff out. Let your passions come at you out of left field while you're otherwise engaged in being curious. And when passion embraces you, commit to it, and develop the heck out of it.

With the next exercise, get clear on the work that inspires and energizes you, that you're endlessly fascinated by and hopelessly besotted with. Give yourself the gift of time to reflect on where your passions lie.

OWN IT

What Are You Passionate About?

Reflect on one or more of these questions:

- What feeds your soul and doesn't feel like work?
- What work-related causes do you care deeply about?
- What are you insatiably curious about?
- What is the work that fuels you?
- Reflect on the peak moments in your career. What were you doing?
- What do you enjoy doing that you could develop passion for?

WHAT DOES YOUR ORGANIZATION VALUE?

Here's what not to do. Don't try to center your professional life on work you're passionate about that draws on your strengths.

Yes, you read that correctly.

Don't build a career around your strengths and passions. If you do, there's a chance you might accidentally end up not with a career but an expensive hobby. I don't want that for you, and I doubt that's what you want that for yourself. Leave that to your friend with the cat aromatherapy business. We both want you to have a long, fulfilling, thrilling career.

If you want a career—a thriving, sustainable career—this third element is a must-have: providing a service that your employer values. Your organization won't sit up and take notice, and you won't be relevant and sought after, unless you're offering something that it needs, wants, and values.

DO WORK THAT'S VALUABLE AND UNDERSTOOD

"The case was *Vista Chemical Company v. the Louisiana Department of Revenue*," says Feeding America CEO Claire Babineaux-Fontenot. "I remember it as though it were yesterday." The case was a high-profile one with a significant impact for the state of Louisiana, but everybody had conceded that it was a loser. At the time, as the most junior lawyer on her team at the Department of Revenue, Claire had been practicing law for a grand total of four months. Ordinarily someone so green would not get a shot at working on a case like this one, but nobody else wanted to touch it.

"I evaluated the situation very differently than my peers or even my superiors because I didn't see any downside," says Claire. If she lost the case, everybody would blame it on the nature of the case itself. She won the case, and it became a defining moment in her career.

In the years since, Claire's role has changed many times, but how she approaches her work has not. She says, "I consider it my imperative to use whatever my personal resources are for the improvement of my organization. I'm constantly asking myself, 'How do I serve my company better?' Making my expertise and accomplishments visible is fundamental to answering that question," she says. At the time we spoke, Claire was partway through a 13-year stint at one of the world's largest retailers, where she was global treasurer, prior to joining Feeding America.

Making great things happen can give an instant boost to your credibility. But before going all-in to deliver something momentous, check that what you're trying to accomplish is genuinely valued. You'll need to understand what your organization values, and how you can apply your talents to help it get there, says Claire. If that's not obvious to you, devote some serious time to finding out. Here are some places to dig.

"What are the growth initiatives of the company?" Katherine Durham encourages you to research. "And where might the company be struggling?" Pay attention to big problems that other people in your organization are fearful of or that they're avoiding dealing with. Embrace them as opportunities where you can make a difference. Could you be the one to fill a leadership gap?

Katherine recommends some ways to learn more about what your organization needs:

- Ask what's important to your boss, your boss's boss, and other key players around you.
- Show up to executive briefings and management talks.
- Listen to investor relations calls.

- Read financial statements.
- Volunteer for special initiatives that are cross-departmental or companywide, where they need representatives from different areas.

Make sure your organization sees where you drive value, a theme we'll revisit in Chapters 6 and 7. Even before Claire Babineaux-Fontenot had a team to lead, she focused on making sure the work she contributed was valuable and that the value was understood. You and your organization co-own the responsibility of helping your organization understand what you can contribute, she says. "If my company doesn't know who I am and doesn't understand what I can do, then it can't possibly know when and where to utilize me effectively."

The next exercise will encourage you to contemplate what do you do, or what you *could* do, to drive value that goes beyond your job title and elevates the success of your organization.

OWN IT

What Does Your Organization Value?

To identify how you can be an invaluable asset to your organization, ask yourself these questions:

- Is my work fully aligned with my organization's strategy?
- Where is my organization trying to go, and how can I help it get there?
- What services can I provide that are valued and sought after?

OUTSOURCE IT

What Does Your Organization Value?

Set up one-on-one time with leaders who are familiar with your strengths and know what you have to contribute, like your mentor, manager, or other leaders. Ask them, "Based on what you know of my strengths, what services can I provide that our organization most needs and values?"

WHAT'S YOUR LEADERSHIP NICHE?

Now for the most important exercise in the book—drumroll—defining your leadership niche, your number 1 superpower.

Grab a mug of your favorite hot beverage, cozy up in your favorite thinking spot, and get ready to tap into that magnificent brain of yours. Here's how it works:

"First, understand where you are in terms of your strengths and passions," says Katherine Durham. "Then identify what your company's needs are. Map out what you have to offer, what the company needs, and what's in that sweet spot—the intersection." In communicating this to others, especially to your management, you'll make yourself incredibly valuable.

Why is nailing down your niche so important? Well, when you figure this out, many of the other career challenges you're struggling with resolve themselves. When you know your niche, you'll know which projects to volunteer for, which roles to say yes to, and which ones to diplomatically decline (and refer to a colleague because it's in *that person's* niche.) When you know your niche, you'll know whom to enlist as your mentors and sponsors. You'll be clearer on which new skills to acquire and additional training or qualifications to undertake. Every career decision becomes a whole a lot easier to tackle when you know your niche.

> **When you know your niche, you'll know which projects to volunteer for, which roles to say yes to, and which ones to diplomatically decline (and refer to a colleague because it's in *that person's* niche.)**

Best of all, when you spot a business gap, problem, or need that's in your sweet spot, you can roll up your sleeves, clip on your Superwoman cape, and spring into action.

Here are some examples from my workshop alumni who've found their niches:

- The aircraft maintenance manager who is constantly looking for ways to drive change and evolve how her team works
- The marketing director who moved to sales, then back to marketing, and now uses that experience to get sales and marketing working together as one team
- The product manager who has designated herself as "the customer's champion"
- The business analytics manager who uncovers the "stories" the data is telling, bringing customers' problems to her organization's attention
- The director for a clinical laboratory who is passionate about science, accuracy, and details.

Identifying and owning your niche can also be healing. Take it from me, the world's most mediocre talent manager turned globe-traipsing evangelist for women's leadership. Claiming your niche gives you permission to spackle over the cracks of past career failures and hurts, so you can paint a far glossier future.

In the previous exercises in this chapter, you described your strengths, your passions, and the value you contribute to your organization. Now we're going to bring it all together by identifying where all three elements intersect.

OWN IT

What's Your Leadership Niche?

What's *your* niche, where one or more of your strengths and passions meet up with something your organization needs?

1. Are you working it today? If so, make some notes. Try to capture your niche in a single sentence, like the five examples from the workshop alumni above.
2. If not, consider the niche you'd like to land in after your next career move, and capture those thoughts in writing.
3. Memorialize your niche in another sticky note, screensaver, or popup reminder, as a daily reminder to guide your actions and decisions.

Was the exercise easy or hard? Did you have any epiphanettes? If it felt easy, or you already knew the answer, then congrats. Some people go a lifetime without discovering theirs. Many of the people who complete this exercise don't figure out their niche at first glance. If you're struggling, don't feel discouraged. Revisit this concept in a day or in a week.

OUTSOURCE IT

What's Your Leadership Niche?

If this exercise feels difficult, outsource it to your close colleagues or a mentor who knows you well. Explain the concept, and ask what *they* think your ideal career niche is. Chances are, they already know but didn't think to tell you.

PLANT YOURSELF WHERE YOU'LL BLOOM

Here comes the single most important tough love tip you'll read here: if you're not currently in a role or organization where you're doing work that you enjoy and are good at, for goodness' sake, don't avoid confronting the mismatch.

You must plant yourself where you'll bloom and thrive, even if it requires uprooting. This encompasses anything from minor tweaks to your role, a campaign to be the one to lead a particular project, or a full-scale career reboot. Every time you get to make a career choice, try to maneuver closer to your niche.

> **Every time you get to make a career choice, try to maneuver closer to your niche.**

You can't begin to grow, lead, climb, and thrive unless your ladder is against the right building.

You've got to be in the role (and ultimately on a career path) where you can dwell in your niche every day.

FIND YOUR LANE

Note: You can't identify your niche today and be done forever. Your environment is constantly changing, and so are you. What your organization and industry need will keep shifting for many reasons, including innovation, disruption, or consolidation. You'll bloom and grow into new strengths and passions too.

I recommend you review the three essential elements—strengths, passions, and value—of your leadership niche every six months or when a major change occurs in your situation or organization. Reevaluate your approach so that you can remain relevant. To have the most rewarding career possible, while making the biggest difference, target roles or assignments that hit the bull's-eye where your strengths, passions, and value overlap.

If you lead people, or aspire to, imagine what a team might be capable of when every team member is operating within the right niche and teammates' strengths complement each other. Beyond that, imagine the power of a team or an entire organization that is collectively engaged in world-class work that it is deeply passionate about and that drives economic success.[4] It's hard to imagine a more energizing place to work. So keep adjusting, do your best to find your lane, and enjoy the ride.

STANDING OUT IS EASIER THAN YOU THINK

You're going to have to trust me on this, but standing out is going to be a lot easier than you think. You don't need to be the foremost thinker or leader in your profession. You need to carve out a valuable niche as a leader. Identify a need or gap that you're passionate about and qualified to fill, and apply your distinctive leadership strengths and character strengths to address it.

If you're a resident expert in your workplace, work to become a rising star outside of it too. If you're already a rising star, aim for industry rock star status. Or better yet, become the iconic, respected go-getter or game changer that your younger self would fangirl over or walk across hot coals to have as a mentor.

That's it.

You don't have to be *the* authority to be *an* authority.

You don't need to be the world's best to make a world of difference.

CHAPTER 3 WRAP-UP

Congratulations. You've conquered Part I and the first three steps.

- You've acknowledged the ways in which you're already a leader (Chapter 1).
- You've identified your standout strengths (Chapter 2).
- You've defined a solid leadership niche (Chapter 3).

The exercises in this chapter helped you identify (or come closer to understanding) your leadership niche—the sweet spot where your standout strengths line up with work that you love to do *and* is a valuable asset to your organization. With your ladder up against the right building, you're in position and ready to lead, rise, and shine.

Here's another way to look at it: You identified your personal awesome-sauce recipe. Next, in Part II (Chapters 4 to 7), you'll get to bottle that special sauce and label it with a description that the world finds irresistible. "Up-leveling" your personal brand statement will promote your value in a way that makes your organization sit up and pay attention. You'll also make a mindset shift from doing to leading, lock in credibility with career-making projects or roles, and make your leadership brand and accomplishments visible so you're not the best-kept secret.

Building an Influential Brand

PART II

In this part, you'll answer the question, "How can I change how others perceive me as a leader?"

I know you're busy, so you will also free up time by letting go of a "doer" mentality as you shift your focus to leading.

Then, you can make yourself and your brand known in ways that make your organization sit up and pay attention.

The next four chapters that make up Part II will help you reinvent how others perceive you and present yourself as the talented emerging leader you are:

- *Chapter 4, Boss Up Your Brand: Up-level How You're Perceived.* Does your personal brand do full justice to your future aspirations? Here, you'll craft a leadership brand statement that stands for something bigger than you can accomplish alone—and lands like "bam."

- *Chapter 5, Get Your Shift Together: Shift Your Mindset from Doing to Leading.* If you aspire to make a bigger impact than you can make alone, you'll need to think and act less like a doer, and more like a leader. Bring your leadership brand to life, by shifting your mindset and behavior.

- ***Chapter 6, Go Big or Go Home: Create Career-Defining Moments.*** A well-chosen, high-profile role or project can propel you to new heights, but the opportunities you say no to will be as important as those you accept. Learn to recognize opportunities that showcase your leadership brand.

- ***Chapter 7, Amplify Your Accomplishments: Don't Be the Best-Kept Secret.*** Don't fall for the myth that your work speaks for itself. Make your leadership brand and key accomplishments visible, while avoiding the common ways self-promotion can backfire.

Boss Up
Your Brand

Up-Level How You're Perceived

> *Be authentic about your own leadership style.*
> *Don't try to change it. Own it. Communicate it.*
> *Put a value on it. Put a brand on it.*
> **—Rohini Anand, PhD,**
> senior vice president, corporate responsibility and
> global chief diversity officer, Sodexo

We need to talk about personal branding.

I'm sure you've already read and heard a lot about why you should have a personal brand. It's inescapable. Google "how to" and "personal brand," and you can dive into thousands of articles on how to develop yours with 5 (or 15 or 26) steps, pillars, or golden rules. The thing is, they all jump straight from "You need to be memorable" to a tactical listicle that says, "Get a website, start a blog, and make sure your LinkedIn profile matches your Twitter headline."

Plus, a lot of what you've seen before was borrowed from marketing principles perfected by fat-budgeted corporations and then slimmed down for small business owners and entrepreneurs. It doesn't take into account how the corporate career climb works, how your brand should evolve over the course of a career, and where you might be getting stuck. These are just a few of the reasons why the listicles come up short.

That lack of real-world, effective guidance is what led me to sift through hundreds of examples of how aspiring and seasoned leaders have branded themselves, intentionally or not. I've come to the conclusion that it's essential to have a branding strategy that takes into account how perceptions must shift and evolve over the course of a career, so that how you're perceived doesn't shortchange your potential. If your personal brand doesn't grow along with you, it can hold you back.

In this chapter, you'll build a real-world, world-class, bomb-ass brand (or bomb-arse, as we Aussies prefer to say).*[1] You'll start by getting a baseline of how you're perceived at work, and then you'll design a leadership brand statement that highlights you as the go-to influencer in the niche you identified in Part I. Let's get to it.

INFLUENCE HOW THEY SEE YOU

Alice Katwan's father immigrated to San Francisco at age 14 to work in his uncle's grocery store. By 16, he had saved enough to bring his parents and four siblings to join him. Now a high-tech sales exec, Alice says, "My father gave me the courage and motivation to pursue my professional aspirations and taught me the value of hard work." Alice made her first foray into sales selling Sunday newspapers on a corner near her home. Three decades later, she's still in sales—and thriving. "The correlation between hard work and clear measurement for success resonated strongly with me," she says. "The sales figures say it all. You're not judged subjectively."

Early in her career, as an individual contributor, Alice was named the most valuable player (MVP) multiple times and was offered opportunities to manage sales teams. Initially, though, she turned down promotions because she had three young boys, and the timing wasn't right for her. Rather than holding her back, Alice says deferring those moves allowed her time to immerse in building the strategic, financial, and leadership skills she would eventually need to lead a large sales organization.

The turning point in her career came when her kids reached a certain level of independence. When all three were old enough to bike to school,

---

* Bomb-ass, *adjective*. Definition: To be extremely good or cool, almost at a godly level of cool. (Urban Dictionary.)

Alice moved into management. "You don't have to choose between being a mom and a kick-ass exec," she wrote in an article for *Working Mother*.[2]

That's not to say it was an easy transition from high-performing team player to manager. As a first-time leader, Alice found it challenging to build credibility with employees and leaders. "When you're promoted from within the ranks, people still see you as an individual contributor," says Alice. "You have to influence how they see you as a manager and establish credibility with accomplishments and maturity. It takes time. You have to start early on."

As Alice settled into her role as a manager, she found a new equilibrium between holding people accountable, making firm decisions, and becoming more of an advisor. Soon, she stood out for her natural ability to mentor, motivate, and develop her people. In helping them achieve their goals, she established herself as a pro at building and leading high-performing teams.

Then came an exhausting, blowout year. "Trying to 'do it all' as a road warrior and working mom literally made me sick," says Alice. Her manager saw her struggling to directly manage a large sales team and laid it on the line: Alice had to become more strategic and concede day-to-day management to the leaders who reported to her. This meant trusting and enabling them, which was a big challenge but one that Alice knew was necessary in order to continue to grow. She went on to lead a team of 120 people who generated 50 percent of her company's revenue for North America, and she became known for building a culture where success breeds success. Now, Alice is senior vice president of North America sales at Salesforce.

Stepping back gave Alice bandwidth to round out her knowledge of the business and raise her profile across the company as a strategic executive. She went on to represent global sales on cross-functional committees and at customer advisory board meetings. She focused on raising her profile outside her company too, with board appointments, advisory roles, speaking at industry events, and as a commencement speaker at her alma mater. "These activities strengthened my brand and how others perceived me as a leader," she says. "I gained confidence and clear direction of where I want to take my career." Her goal is the C-suite.

"Don't 'fake it 'til you make it,'" Alice says. Instead, prove to yourself that you can be it. Look for something that influences your ability to feel confident. "There have been several milestones in my career where I've had that 'aha' moment and thought, 'Wow, I can do this,' she says. "Confidence will take you wherever you want to go. With it, you'll be able to build your brand and take your career to the next level."

Alice purposefully took steps to publicly reveal her leadership skills and executive potential. There's more to you than people see too. Year in and year out, you work hard to evolve your leadership skills and elevate your impact, but the way the rest of the world perceives you won't always keep pace.

It's not enough to *be* it if no one can *see* it. You'll need to reinvent how others see you too. This is one of the most important lessons in the book,

> **It's not enough to *be* it if no one can *see* it.**

and creating your own leadership brand statement—the focus of this chapter—holds the key to your success.

YOU ALREADY HAVE A BRAND

Dr. Neeli Bendapudi has researched how open customers are to developing long-term loyalties to companies and their brands. She's also a charismatic, spirited ambassador for the value of developing a well-honed personal brand, as she explained when she joined me for a webinar interview.

We are confronted with more choices than we know what to do with in every sphere of our lives, says Neeli, president of the University of Louisville. "When you walk down a supermarket aisle, how do you make your decisions?" she asks. "Do you look at all 50 cereal brands, compare the boxes, and then decide what you want?" No, you go by the brand because it has certain attributes that you've grown to rely on. And this, she explains, is the crux of why it's so important to have a well-defined brand in your professional life. "A brand is a way to stand out in a sea of similarity," says Neeli. "If you want to be memorable and be remembered for having certain unique attributes, to be sought out, and to be an employee of choice, then you must manage your personal brand."

Here's one of the most important things to realize: *you already have a personal brand.*

You might not be aware of it because you did not create it.

The people you work with have "branded" you in their own minds.

They have formed opinions about what you're good at, but it's not the full, vivid account of all you have to offer: your strengths, value, and potential. It's a fuzzier image, filtered through brief interactions, hearsay, assumptions, and biases. They might hold *favorable* perceptions, but most of the people you work with haven't studied in detail what you're awesome at and imagined what you'll be great at next. That's your job. Don't outsource it to people who may have their own agenda.

Everyone has a brand. Most people have one by default. Yours should be built by design.

"Perception is the copilot to reality" declared Carla Harris, vice chair, managing director, and senior client advisor at Morgan Stanley, in her keynote at a MAKERS Conference.[3] "How people perceive you will directly impact how they deal with you." Your ability to ascend will be a function of someone else's judgment, she says, pointing out all of the important decisions about your career that will be made when you are not in the room. Says Carla:

> **Everyone has a brand. Most people have one by default. Yours should be built by design.**

> Compensation decisions will be made when you are not in the room.
> Promotion decisions will be made when you are not in the room.
> New assignments will be given out when you are not in the room.

To influence how you're spoken of when you aren't in the room, you need to seize control of this narrative.

GET A BASELINE OF YOUR BRAND

Day in, day out, you hustle from meeting to meeting, field incoming updates and action items, and stay on top of deliverables. Did you remember to eat lunch and drink enough water, but not *too* much? (No time for extra restroom breaks.) Somehow, you find time to move mountains and get sh!t done. But when was the last time you paused to take a pulse on your personal brand?

Start by acknowledging how little you really know. "Everyone understands what it feels like to be misunderstood," says Heidi Grant, chief science officer with the NeuroLeadership Institute.[4] What is surprising, she says, is how remarkably inept we are at gauging the extent to which we're misperceived and misunderstood. "It's a lot more than we realize," says Heidi.

How do people describe you when you're not in the room?

If you're not entirely clear, that's OK. The next two exercises are designed to get you a more accurate read. Only 35 percent of individual contributors and midlevel managers I polled admitted that they know and like how they are perceived.[5] This can be turned around with a stunningly simple yet effective question, if you're courageous enough to ask it.

"If you're willing to try this, it can be quite eye opening," says Heidi. "Ask someone who knows you well to fill in the blank: "If I didn't know you better, I would think that you were _____." For example, you might hear, "If I didn't know you better, I would think you were <u>aloof</u>."

OUTSOURCE IT

What's Your Baseline Brand?

Dare to enlist at least five people, such as your most trusted colleagues, managers, and mentors:

- Let them know you're on a mission to increase self-awareness of how you're perceived at work. Ask them to complete this sentence as honestly as possible: "If I didn't know you better, I would think that you were _____."
- Want to dig deeper? Ask:
  - How am I perceived by people on our team? Outside of our team?
  - How do people describe me when I'm not around?
  - What's my personal brand at work?

When you're done, give yourself a fist bump. It takes courage to ask for and be open to honest critique.

Analyze what you discovered or talk it out with a confidant. How do the perceptions you gathered square with what you anticipated or wanted to hear?

OWN IT

What's Your Baseline Brand?

Now fold it all together. What is your actual, real-time personal brand today? Write your responses to these questions as honestly as you can:

- What am I currently known for?
- How do people describe me when I'm not in the room?

Don't skimp on these exercises. When you're able to view yourself as others perceive you, you have the ammo to make a powerful choice: embrace and amplify that image, or disrupt and redefine it.

TAKE CHARGE OF YOUR CAREER TRAJECTORY

It's no understatement to say that a clear and compelling brand statement can shift an entire career trajectory. Here are two of my favorite examples.

From High Maintenance to Excellence

A quality assurance engineer with a manufacturing company approached me for some personal coaching. Chelsea had been acknowledged as a high performer, but she was getting overlooked for expanded responsibilities. Wanting to understand why, she launched a 360-degree feedback survey.* What she discovered devastated her: she was considered "high maintenance."

Chelsea opened up about what had gone wrong. She was the only one on her team who paid attention to details and set high standards. She was

---

* A *360-degree*, or *multirater*, *feedback survey* is a tool for gathering and aggregating performance feedback from a variety of sources, such as peers, subordinates, and supervisors.

unafraid of calling out problems that others might be inclined to over-look. But when she spoke up, Chelsea encountered resistance and defensiveness. It didn't matter that she was often right. She looked crushed with the weight of feeling misunderstood.

Thinking out loud, I observed that she seemed to have *a passion for excellence*. Chelsea's face lit up. "That's what I want my brand to be!" she exclaimed. She quickly drew up a list of actions to avoid because they triggered her team's defensiveness and other actions that would show she was on their side as a passionate champion for excellence.

From Master of None to Master Strategist

Anastasia had jumped from department to department during her decade at a solar energy equipment manufacturer. She started out in engineering, spent time in product design, and then raised her hand to lead a large-scale transformation initiative. When it concluded, she landed, unhappily, in finance, until the head of IT noticed and gave her an IT program to roll out. Anastasia was known as "Jill of all trades, master of none" in a company that promoted leaders who had owned one functional area or department.

"Career ADHD?" Anastasia responded when I asked what brand she was currently known for. Reviewing her history and most satisfying experiences, Anastasia searched for the common thread. Turns out, she was relentlessly drawn toward chaotic situations in which she could identify an effective strategy to solve a problem, lead the development of a turnaround plan, and rally a team around it. But as soon as the plan was underway, she'd feel antsy and start to scan the organization for another chaotic situation.

Her company had a leadership gap, one that she was uniquely qualified to close. She decided to position herself as *the go-to leader for corporate strategy*, and she volunteered to facilitate strategy conversations for other department heads. They quickly realized that if strategy was ever being discussed, Anastasia needed to be at the whiteboard, facilitating. She wrote a proposal to the CEO to create an office of corporate strategy. "By the way," she quipped, "I know the ideal person to lead it."

Each misperception exacts its price. Misstep 4 is *allowing others to define your reputation.*

Designing how you want to be perceived is the Leaderly Move to replace it with. If you've gotten stuck with a negative reputation, or one that downplays all that you're capable of, there's hope! You *can* shake it off. It takes time and whopping bucketloads of focus, but it's eminently doable. As Carla Harris points out, you can train people to think about you in the way that you want to be thought of.[6]

IS YOURS A LEADERSHIP BRAND?

You already have a brand. But does it do full justice to your future aspirations?

If your existing personal brand is not communicating the sum of all that you're capable of—or your value and distinctiveness as a leader—you're not alone.

Reimagine Your Brand and Advocate It into Reality is the title of a series of conference keynotes and corporate workshops that I cofacilitated with Selena Rezvani. In the lead-up to one conference, we gathered survey responses from 230 women leaders from director level to the C-suite at companies of all sizes, from scrappy startups to global behemoths. As the responses came in, a fascinating pattern took shape. When asked to evaluate the statement, "I'm satisfied with the personal brand that I'm most known for today," 60 percent agreed.[7] But get this: when asked whether their current personal brand conveys their *full leadership potential*, that figure was slashed in half. That ratio has remained consistent across similar groups we've since surveyed.

Put another way, 70 percent of established women leaders felt they were perceived as less adept at leading than they were willing and able to prove. Going by appearances, these seasoned, influential women looked to be at top of their game. But still they felt underestimated, undervalued, possibly even overlooked.

Do you?

You already have a brand, but is it a *leadership* brand?

The takeaway, which isn't altogether surprising, is that having a great

> **You already have a brand, but is it a *leadership* brand?**

brand isn't good enough if it sells you short. Ask yourself, does my personal brand accurately convey my leadership potential?

MAKE YOUR BRAND SCALABLE

Krista Thomas, senior vice president and global head of marketing for VideoAmp, has built a career helping companies build influential brands as they scale to serve a growing customer base. She also offers similar career advice that landed on me like a truthbomb with a slow-burning fuse the first time she said it: "You must make your personal brand scalable too."

A scalable business is one that's growing and expanding its impact while laying down the infrastructure for future, exponential growth. You wouldn't want to work for a company that was unable to scale, so don't settle for a personal brand that limits your growth prospects. Krista's notion of a scalable personal brand rapidly seared itself into my brain, and I've been thinking, writing, and speaking about it ever since. This insight was one of the sparks that got me fired me up about writing this book: make your brand scalable.

Krista is a striking case in point. When we first met, she was the communications director with a Silicon Valley search engine, poised to make a pivotal career shift. She was smashing it at the rank-and-file corporate communications work like investor relations presentations and securing media coverage. This got her to where she was but wasn't going to take her further. Krista was dreaming up a new chapter in her career: one with less doing, more leading, and a foreseeable path into senior leadership. She made a career sidestep into marketing management, and by the next time we spoke, she had landed her first VP-level marketing role with a global news and information service.

Around that time, Krista made a guest appearance in one of my webinars (and brought the illustrious "scalable brand" quote). I asked her what her own brand statement was, and she explained, "Passionate evangelist and advocate for my organization's products." She was known for passion and commitment to new ideas, her domain expertise and industry knowledge, and her ability to make something complicated clear and compelling.

Having landed the leap from doing to leading, Krista was thinking deeply about what could make for a satisfying next step. She did a creative visualization around the role she saw herself in. "I asked myself, 'How do I mold myself into the type of executive that CEOs and CTOs turn to for counsel? How can I put myself in a leadership role where I'm building a team instead of doing the hands-on work?'" says Krista. She plotted a strategy to get into her first senior executive leadership position, where she could build a department from the ground up.

"We're trained to want to stay safe and move toward established career paths where we won't have to worry about stability or risks. Unfortunately, that doesn't always match up with what you aspire to do," says Krista. Realizing her goal took a move to Los Angeles where she built departments from scratch, initially for a small startup and then with a larger company that was about to go public.

In remaking herself from rank-and-file corporate communications "doer" to a passionate evangelist for her organization's products, to the marketer that C-suite leaders turn to for counsel and growth strategies, Krista was able to elevate her brand and accelerate her climb.

How will you know when it's time to reenvision your brand? Anytime you catch yourself getting intellectually bored, uninspired, or less than challenged, says Krista. "Anytime you have reached your goal, it is time to set a bigger goal."

Who do you want to be and what do you want to be doing three years from now? That's a question you answered in Chapter 1, when you dreamed big and created a bold, lofty goal. Work backward from that point, and imagine the reputation you'll need to cultivate *now* to enable that future. That's how you make your brand scalable.

BOSS UP YOUR BRAND

For your personal brand to remain in step with your current skill level, it must grow—or "boss up"—along with you. Krista Thomas achieved this. She started out executing rank-and-file corporate communications work and developed into "a passionate evangelist and advocate her organization's products." She is now known as "the marketing executive that CEOs and CTOs turn to for counsel."

What does "boss up" mean? It means evolving how you're perceived—"up-leveling" your brand, to represent your ability to operate like a boss at the next tier of leadership. How do you reinvent yourself for a big leap forward in your career? As Krista says, you must make that brand of yours *scalable*: a growth-accelerating brand.

You'll know you've outgrown your existing brand when you're repeatedly offered the types of roles, assignments, and tasks that you would have gone bonkers with excitement about in the past. But now, you feel underestimated. Undervalued. You're ready to make a mightier contribution, but the people you work with remain none the wiser.

MISSTEP 5

Misstep 5 is *getting stuck with a dead-end brand*—one that stifles your growth and holds you back.

The Leaderly Move is *making your brand scalable*. In the remainder of this chapter, you'll dream up a personal brand that fuels your passion, signals your value, and embodies your aspirations.

Entry-Level Brands

When you first entered the workforce, you probably recognized the importance of building a strong entry-level brand. You landed your first job and hit the ground running, showing that there's real substance to what you offer. You might have heard phrases like these, which show up in descriptions of solid, prized, early-career players:

- Valued contributor
- Team player
- Tactical executor
- Gets sh!t done
- Specialist
- Go-to person

If you're kicking off your career and you want to start strong, go after being talked about in terms like these. Any of them will serve you well. But if you're three, four, or more years into your career and are still being referred to by one of these entry-level terms, that perception is now holding you back (like Tina, whose journey from team-playing pooper-scooper to change agent I shared in the Introduction). Breaking away is not a given. Even today, women are 21 percent less likely than men to be promoted beyond entry level, with women of color facing a steeper climb.[8]

"I am in a role that is below my skill set," said one of my workshop participants. Said another, "I would love to be perceived as more of a leader, to rise above my reputation of being a solid contributor and execution master."

Think about it: Do people come to you with requests that underestimate your abilities? Is the perception that you're still "junior" implicit in what's asked of you? If so, your potential has eclipsed your brand. It's time to boss up how you're perceived. An entry-level brand describes someone who is squarely focused on *doing* work, not leading it. Don't get me wrong—that's a tremendous asset to any team, but it's not how people rise. Is it time for you to construct your springboard by cultivating a more leaderly brand: a midlevel brand that undeniably declares your "badass bosslady" status?

Midlevel Brands

Leadership calls for making a larger impact than you can make alone, and a midlevel brand tells the story of someone who's making the move from doing to leading. No longer solo performers, leaders at this level engage, inspire, and motivate others to collaborate with them. They're daring to effect a bigger difference than one individual can. They spend part of their time delivering solo work and part leading others.

Here are some phrases that epitomize successful midlevel professionals:

- People motivator
- Project leader
- Team catalyst
- Strategist

- Results driver
- Fixer
- Process improver
- Customers' champion
- Subject matter expert
- Innovator

If any of these examples sound similar to how you'd like to be described, highlight them or write them down.

Senior-Level Brands

You'll arrive at the next inflection point as an established midlevel leader, capable of leading more broadly, but the upper echelon of middle management is where many careers stall. "I have a great brand at work," said one conference attendee, "but it's a great brand for my current role and level. I need to polish it to come across at a higher level than I am today." Another, known for her open, friendly demeanor, said "I want to go from being known as 'personable' to being seen as capable and effective at running a business in a medium to large org."

Is it time for you to audaciously boss up to a senior-level brand? Here are some descriptors that are frequently applied to seasoned leaders:

- Leader who develops leaders
- Culture catalyst
- Big picture leader
- Makes big things happen
- Turnaround architect
- Transformational leader
- Dealmaker
- Thought leader
- Visionary

Do any of these words or phrases resonate with you? Could they form a part of your own brand statement? If so, highlight them or write them down.

Here are examples of how other leaders have made the shift from doing to leading, and how to plot your course from an early-career brand to one that reflects how you want to be spoken of when you're not in the room:

- Having initially being known for "getting things done," Kathy Tyra from Chapter 1 grew into a self-described "operations geek." Now, as an operations executive, she's "a business transformer who quickly creates calm out of chaos and develops long-term strategic plans."
- In the next chapter, I tell the story of Dona Munsch and how her career took off when she recast herself from "the get-'er-done gal" to an "influencer" and ultimately an "enabler," a creator of environments in which others were enabled to accomplish great things.
- Nina Bhatti, whose story appears in Chapter 6, started her career as an engineer with an uncanny knack for spotting and fixing unmet needs, and she became "a technologist who discovers opportunities, then engineers technical breakthroughs."

Think of the entirety of your career as a series of evolutions of your brand. Each inflection point ushers in a challenging new career phase. Sometimes shifts happen naturally (if you're lucky). Other times, they happen through conscious reinvention because you're bored, too comfortable, underutilized, or ready for a new challenge. As author Lalah Delia has said, "If you are outgrowing who you've been, you are right on schedule. Keep evolving."[9]

OWN IT

How Has Your Brand Evolved?

Reflect on your career to date, and answer the following questions:
- What brand were you known for when you started out your career?
- Is that different from what you're known as now?
- Are you overdue for a change?

50 LEADERSHIP BRAND STATEMENTS

Want even more real-life examples? For over a decade, I've been encouraging the people who attend my keynotes, workshops, and webinars to dream big, boss up, and boldly declare their brand identities. Six thousand program participants. Ten years of collecting and curating brand statements. Fifty stand-out examples.

Here are the most memorable—the ones I'd love you to borrow, adapt, build on, or be inspired by. They're representative of all career levels and a smattering of every imaginable industry. They've come from professionals, mostly women, in North America, Europe, and Asia-Pacific. Sorted by the five core leader types (as we discussed in Chapter 1), these are standout examples to draw inspiration from when you create your own:

Change Leader Brands
- Transformation strategist
- Master disruptor
- Fixer and firefighter
- Process evolver
- Catalyst for future-forward change
- Transformer of struggling engineering organizations
- Complexity calmer
- Champion of efficiency and continual improvement
- Evolutionary change leader
- Turnaround architect for new technologies

People Leader Brands
- Talent whisperer
- Transformational people catalyst
- Developer of the next generation of leaders
- Team healer
- Culture shifter
- Passionate culture catalyst
- Compassionate fearless leader
- Quiet, thoughtful leader
- Charismatic peacemaker
- Cross-team bridge builder

Results Leader Brands

- Enabler, influencer, and motivator
- Unleasher of team energy
- Builder of a culture where success breeds success
- Organizational productivity maximizer
- Game changer
- Problem identifier, problem solver, and problem preventer
- Deliverer of data-driven customer-oriented results
- Closer of big business deals
- Passionate "goal-getter"
- Leader of teams that accomplish big dreams

Service Leader Brands

- Leader of change inspired by customers
- Force that drives customer championship
- Deliverer of delightful consumer experiences
- Customer trust advocate
- Uniter of technology and people, in service of customers
- Passionate driver of outstanding design that users love and value
- Healer of what's broken
- Ambassador for ideas that change or improve our society
- Social justice executive
- Warrior for a better life for the patient

Thought Leader Brands

- Trendsetter, barrier breaker, and innovation maker
- Innovator who creates winning strategies
- Transformer of data into innovation
- Innovation architect
- Intrapreneur* that scales from startup to rainmaker
- Trend spotter
- Negotiation strategist
- Strategic communications architect
- Knowledge cascader
- Visionary product leader

---

* Intrepreneurs act entrepreneurially while working within a large company. They innovate and bring new products to market, adding profitable new areas of business.

OK, I couldn't resist. Here are two more that made me exclaim, "Damn, that's memorable":

- Badass inspirational B.S. eliminator
- Bomb diggity change ranger

Want more? Head to www.jomiller.com/brands to get your list of 100 brand statements.

. . .

You already have a brand, but it's not a leadership brand unless it speaks of how you stand for something bigger than you can accomplish alone.

By completing the exercises in Chapter 3, you've identified your *leadership niche*, the point of harmony between your strengths, passions, and value. In the next exercise, you'll distill it into one sentence—a succinct, compelling bossed-up brand statement that bridges the gap between where you are and your leadership aspirations and sums up how you want to be spoken of when you're not in the room.

OWN IT

Boss up Your Brand

1. In Chapter 3, you identified your leadership niche, the point of harmony between your strengths, passions, and value. Read yours again to get grounded in the source of your unique value before moving to the next step.

2. Read the list of 50 brand statements, looking for words or phrases that resonate with you. Highlight them or write them down. Use this list for a starting point and inspiration, but I challenge you to go beyond it. Be wildly imaginative in coming up with your own statement.

3. Next, boss up your brand, to express not just who you are today but your leadership aspirations as well. To do this, return to the goal you identified in Chapter 2, when you dreamed bigger, and set a bold, lofty goal. Work backward from that endpoint, and

---

imagine the brand you'll need to cultivate and become known for *now* to realize your goal.

4. Distill your niche and your goal into one succinct, compelling sentence that sums up how you want to be spoken of when you're not in the room. Something that would look right at home as the headline on your résumé or LinkedIn profile, or on a presentation title slide. *This is your leadership brand statement.* Write it down.

BUILD A BRAND THAT LANDS LIKE BAM

When I interviewed the phenomenal Claire Babinueax-Fontenot, CEO of Feeding America, it was for a webinar about how to not be invisible in your organization. I asked her to describe the personal brand she had carved out for herself. What was she was known for? Claire, who was a senior leader with one of the world's largest retail companies at the time, replied without a moment's hesitation. "I'd like to believe that I'm known as one who identifies, nurtures, and catalyzes talent; who gets things done with courage and compassion," she said. For me, it was one of those instantly unforgettable statements. So much more than a slogan or catchphrase, this was a deeply held conviction about the way she strives to lead.

Would it surprise you to hear that her role at that time was chief tax officer? Claire defined herself and her niche not only by her detailed understanding of tax policy, the Internal Revenue Code, and her contributions to her company's bottom line, but moreover by her passion for being of service and developing others. Here's Claire's advice to anyone else hoping to become that clear: "Know who you are. Go through a proper process of introspection, and understand how it is that you uniquely drive value, and make that your platform."

Does your brand statement convey how you uniquely drive value? To find out, run it by the ultimate test, the three essential elements of an effective niche from Chapter 3:

- Does it describe something your company values? (If not, you're heading for an expensive hobby, not a career.)
- Does it play to your strengths? (Without those, you'll never rise above mediocrity.)
- Does it fuel your passions? (If not, it won't sustain you through a crappy day, let alone a bad quarter.)

Your brand statement has the potential to be much, much more than a sexy marketing catchphrase. If yours is thoughtfully crafted, it can light a fire in your belly. It can be a beacon of inspiration to guide you through transitions and challenges, and it can serve as a constant reminder of all that you're capable of leading and being. Is your brand statement dope . . . or nope?

Here are six ways to elevate and refine your brand statement into one that stands for something bigger than you can accomplish alone—and lands like "bam."

1. Be the Change

Some brand statements describe the kinds of knotty problems that people typically shy away from. Is there a type of challenge that you're drawn to and undaunted by? Refer to it in your brand statement, so there's no mistaking that you offer something greatly needed by your group, company, or customer. This type of brand statement speaks directly to a visceral pain point that is being experienced, and it positions you as the one to lead beyond it. Some examples from the list of 50 brand statements are these:

- Complexity calmer
- Transformer of struggling engineering organizations
- Warrior for a better life for the patient

By incorporating a problem you'll solve or outcome you'll deliver, you're not only articulating your brand. You're delivering a sense of relief as it sinks in, "She's got this handled."

2. Make an Uncommon Match

When GoDaddy's Shradha Balakrishnan left the nonprofit world for private industry, she carried with her a passion for the intersection of social impact and technology. Her brand statement, created a decade ago in one of my workshops, is "Drives social impact through technology solutions that deeply impact peoples' lives."

There's something intriguing about someone whose standout attributes are divergent, seemingly clashing, or rare in their profession. If you can you bridge between disciplines to help salespeople and scientists find common ground, or if you're the lone intuitive on a team of implementers, or a passionate advocate for what data can reveal about patient care, make the most of that mashup. If there's an unconventional combination among your passions or strengths and they fill an underserved need in your organization, make it the basis for a standout brand.

3. Add a Dash of Sass

Did you smile when you read the bonus leadership brands "Bomb diggity change ranger" and "Badass inspirational B.S. eliminator"? The most memorable brands have a dash of sass and moxie thrown in.

A brand statement that makes people smile, lifts the mood, and releases tension in a room can be stealthily influential. A good sense of humor is associated with intelligence,[10] and if you can make people laugh as you deliver an important message, it's more memorable.[11] But you've got to know your audience and what's situation appropriate. If you can pull that off, go for it.

4. Spotlight a Strength of Character

Remember the character strengths from Chapter 2 that differentiate you from others in your profession? They are correlated with greater satisfaction at work.[12] For example, when I asked Claire Babineaux-Fontenot about her brand, she answered "I'd like to believe I'm known as the one who identifies, nurtures, and catalyzes talent; who gets things done with courage and compassion."

Some strong character strengths from the long list of brand statements include these:

- Compassionate fearless leader
- Charismatic peacemaker
- Passionate goal-getter

Is there a singularity of spirit you bring to what you do? Call it out. Adding that strength to your brand statement can make it all the more rare, valuable, and compelling.

5. Have Conviction

Your brand statement can become a beacon that guides you through thorny situations.

When Claire is in the throes of a difficult decision, she will often go back to her brand statement and test her reaction to the situation by asking the question, "Does my reaction measure up to who it is that I represent myself to be?" Claire says, "There have been moments in which I was going to pursue a course that was not particularly courageous but was expedient, and I realized that that was not what I stand for. I regrouped and refocused and proceeded in a way that was more courageous."

If you have deeply held personal values, infuse them into your brand statement so you can speak it with conviction and be reminded of what you care about.

6. Test It on Humans

Not everyone needs to get what you're referring to as long as your message packs a punch for your intended audience. Yes, your brand must make you glow with pride, but it also needs to captivate your constituency. Ask yourself whether your brand statement goes "pow" in their hearts and minds.

The final exercise in this chapter requires testing your brand statement by sharing it with people. Ideally, you'll see them nod in agreement or lean in closer, curiosity piqued. Or they might ask questions, intrigued to learn more. In workshop settings, I've seen 50 heads nod in agreement after hearing a *great* brand statement.

I've also lost count of the number of times I've stood at the front of a training room, listening in on a conversation, as a brand statement goes from hazy to clear in two minutes or less. Overthinking won't get you closer to that kind of clarity, so enlist support from others who can identify the elements that best spotlight your value. If you're not there yet, bounce yours around with a couple of people who know and appreciate what you have to offer. Or run it by someone who has a gift for marketing communications or wordsmithing.

OUTSOURCE IT

Captivate Your Constituency

Test your brand statement out on some people who are part of the population who *should* get it. Watch how they respond.

If necessary, continue to refine the phrasing.

If stuck, bounce it around with people who know and appreciate your worth.

CHAPTER 4 WRAP-UP

Everyone has a brand. Most people have one by default, but yours should be developed by design, or it may stifle your career growth. That's why you must make your brand scalable, starting with your ultimate aspiration, your lofty career or leadership goal, and then imagining the reputation you'll need to cultivate *now* to enable that future.

In this chapter, you took a snapshot of your baseline personal brand—the way you're perceived today. You wrote a new, bossed-up brand statement that represents not only your leadership niche—where your strengths and passions align with the value you bring to your organization—but also your future aspirations. And you did this all in one succinct, compelling sentence that sums up how you want to be spoken of when you're not in the room.

Now it's time make your brand real. In Chapters 5, 6, and 7, you'll bring your brand statement to life with a leader's mindset and accomplishments. No longer an aspiration, that phrase will become how you're actually seen.

5

Get Your Shift Together

Shift Your Mindset from Doing to Leading

> My get-'er-done mentality—as the go-to person,
> and the only one who knew how to do
> certain things—got in my way of moving ahead.
> I couldn't step out of my own role to
> take on new opportunities.
> **—Dona Munsch,**
> former vice president of cloud operations, NetApp

In Chapter 2, you identified your professional, leadership, and character strengths. In Chapter 3, you aligned those strengths with your passions and an organizational need to define your leadership niche. In Chapter 4, you dreamed up a "bossed-up" leadership brand statement that speaks of your desire to deliver bolder, bigger outcomes than you can achieve on your own.

You now have a brand statement—but University of Louisville President Dr. Neeli Bendapudi has a concern about that. "Is it just your aspiration, or is it how you're actually seen?" she asks. "When I hear people speak about building a personal brand, I worry that they have the impression that all we really need to do is come up with a catchy slogan," she says. "But that's the easy part. The more difficult part is how your peers, bosses, and direct reports actually see you."

Your **brand identity**, Neeli explains, describes how you wish to be seen. You might figure out what you're passionate about, you're really good at, and your company currently values, and you might write that in your LinkedIn headline. "Well, great," she quips, "that's your aspiration. That's what you want to be."

But the trick, according to Neeli, is remembering that your brand is not what *you* think you are, it's what *others* think you are. "What matters is the **brand experience** that they take away. Your brand is a dynamic, living entity," says Neeli. "It's the experience others have when they interact with you." Is the brand experienced by people who encounter you consistent with who you aspire to be?

"A brand is a promise," says Neeli. "The power of a brand lies in whether the promise is delivered. It is only as good as whether I live up to that promise." What matters is not what we say, but how we act.

During my interview with Neeli, I must have referred to her as "Dr. Bendapudi" one too many times. She exclaimed, "Jo! Please don't refer to me as Dr. Bendapudi. Neeli is just fine. I hope I'm seen as someone who is accessible. That's part of my brand."

How accessible? Well, when Neeli was appointed president of the University of Louisville, she gave out her personal cell phone number, along with instructions to contact her for any reason, to 1,200 first-year students.[1]

If *your* brand is a promise, how can you make sure to deliver on that aspirational, bossed-up promise?

This chapter is about making a series of key shifts in mindset and behavior so you can show up ready to lead, influence, and make a bigger impact than you can make alone. You'll need to think and act less like a doer and more like a leader, so you're remembered in a way that's consistent with who you aspire to be.

This transition from *doing* to *leading* is one of the trickiest, stickiest shifts to make in a career, but one that's absolutely necessary if you want to launch yourself beyond where you are today.

The tactical skills and talents that have served you well so far *won't* be enough to get you to your next leadership milestone. In fact, if you don't unlearn those success factors to make way for new ones, you might even derail. What got you here definitely won't get you there.

MISSTEP 6

Career Misstep 6 is *acting like a doer, not a leader.*

The Leaderly Move is *shifting your mindset from "me" to "we."* If you aspire to grow beyond a doer role, you'll need to rethink where you focus your attention. To expand your impact beyond what you can accomplish as a solo performer, you've got to do less, lead more, and engage, inspire, and influence others to collaborate with you.

I've broken the process down into five key shifts in mindset and behavior that I call "The Shift List."* If you want to move from doing to leading, here's how you get your shift together:

The Shift List

Shift 1. Tactician to strategist

Shift 2. Doing to delegating

Shift 3. Optimizer to transformer

Shift 4. Order taker to rule breaker

Shift 5. "Me" to "we"

Some shifts will be more relevant to your situation than others, so you won't need to implement them all. As I describe each shift in depth, look for one in particular that represents the most important shift you'll focus on in the next year in order to fulfill your leadership brand's promise.

SHIFT 1. TACTICIAN TO STRATEGIST

"You need to be more strategic" is feedback many leaders—aspiring, new, and seasoned—often hear. Have you ever stopped to wonder what it really means?

---

* The Shift List concept was inspired by conversations with Lisa Walsh who in turn was inspired by Michael D. Watkins, "How Managers Become Leaders," *Harvard Business Review*, June 2012, https://hbr.org/2012/06/how-managers-become-leaders.

Ellie Humphrey has. She's vice president of enterprise excellence and business transformation at Medtronic, but in a previous role, she was responsible for global strategy. So how does a seasoned strategist define *strategy*? Quite simply, as it turns out. Ellie says, "*Strategy* is a fancy word for coming up with a long-term plan and putting it into action."

This matters because being strategic is one of the critical competencies that allow someone with raw potential to develop into a competent leader.[2] Someone like Dona Munsch, for example.

"My father was an incredibly hard worker," says Dona. Inspired by his example at the beginning of her own career, starting out as a project coordinator, she embraced a "just do what needs to be done" work ethic that served her well, at least for a while. "I started out as the ultimate tactician," says Dona. "I had this continuous drive to enjoy the intoxicating buzz of checking off things on my list," she says.

Then came a big wake-up call. Dona spotted a higher-level role she aspired to move into, but she was told that she couldn't take it because nobody knew how to replace her in the role she occupied. She'd been stymied by, of all things, her epic work ethic. "My 'get-'er-done' mentality—as the go-to person, and the only one who knew how to do certain things— got in my way of moving ahead," says Dona. "I couldn't step out of my own role to take on new opportunities."

Does any of this sound familiar?

Dona's experience became the catalyst for her to engineer a major turning point in her career. She reinvented herself from the get-'er-done gal to "influencer"— a midlevel brand. She began to think and act more strategically, influence across departments, and drive more valuable business outcomes. Later, she became NetApp's vice president of cloud operations and evolved her leadership brand to "enabler." In practice, this meant laying the groundwork that enabled the productivity of others, by clarifying the direction, strategy, and values. Dona was there for her team when they needed her, but otherwise got out of the way.

Let's face it, there's something really gratifying about checking tasks off a to-do list. Your boss hands you a project to execute or a problem to solve, and in the completion comes a degree of reward and satisfaction. It's immediately gratifying, but if you aspire to really play big and expand your influence, you'll need to think and act more strategically.

As a practical matter, how do you make the move from being tactical to strategic? Dona recommends three questions you can begin asking yourself immediately, even if you don't have direct reports.

Question 1. What's My Time Horizon?

One difference between tacticians and strategists lies in their time horizon. Shifting your attention away from what's required of you in the near future and focusing on the longer term encourages you to become more forward thinking, visionary, and strategic. If you want to be a strategist, Dona recommends asking yourself every day:

- What is the time horizon for what I'm doing and influencing— today, tomorrow, a year from now, or five years from now?
- Am I being tactical in what I'm doing, focused on today and tomorrow, or am I strategically looking ahead a year or more and influencing what might happen?

Question 2. What's the Scope of My Influence?

By watching how leaders at the next level operated, Dona realized that she did not have to be the one to do something to get it done. "You can accomplish a lot through influence," says Dona.

To expand your scope of influence, look for ways to build new relationships and grow your network. Ask yourself:

- Are you working with only a few team members who report to the same person you do? If so, you're probably being more tactical.
- Are you influencing and working more widely, team to team, or with organizations that are outside of your day-to-day role? This is what strategists do.
- What can you do that could be of value to others? How can you help a person, another team, or the organization be better?

The more you can understand what's important to others and facilitate their success, the more skilled you'll become at engaging them to collaborate with you to make things happen. That's what influencers do.

Question 3. What's the Extent of the Change I'm Driving?

Examine the degree of change that you're driving. A tactician chips away at the kind of goals that don't threaten the status quo or require building new networks or learning new skills. A strategist sets out to create the type of groundbreaking change that requires a completely different way of thinking and operating.

Another element that differentiates tactical execution from strategic action is what Dona calls "irreversible change," a change that can't be undone. So to become more strategic, scale up your aspirations. Go after driving broad, sweeping change. Tell your story of where things are going to be five years from now. Not what needs to be done today or tomorrow, but a more aspirational view.

"When you're talking strategy, long-term goals, and transformational change, your arms should be out wide and moving like you're conducting an orchestra," says Dona. "You can't do that with T-Rex arms." Don't be a tactical T-Rex.

To become a better strategist, *slow the heck down*, if only for an hour or so. Give yourself time to just think. When you're running from meeting to meeting *and* trying to accomplish more in less time, it feels sometimes like there's not even enough time to get your job done. Schedule some quiet, unstructured time to think strategically.

OWN IT

Shifting from Tactician to Strategist

Look at a month on your calendar. Color code your activities and meetings, using one color for tactical pursuits and another for strategic ones.

Ask yourself:

- Which tactical activities could you let go of? Even if it's one or two, that's a solid starting point.
- What would you like to do more of, especially on the strategic side?

Pick one of the three questions asked by strategic leaders (time horizon, scope of influence, or change) to focus on.

Schedule an hour just to think.

SHIFT 2. DOING TO DELEGATING

"The most successful leaders don't try to do it all," says Alice Katwan.

After taking her first director-level sales role, Alice's life became a lot more complex and chaotic. "I thought I could cook dinner every night, keep the house clean, get the laundry done, work full time in the high-stress world of high-tech sales, and make it to three different sporting events on the same day," says Alice. "Oh, and do it all perfectly."

The breaking point came when her health took a nosedive. Says Alice, "I'll never forget the day my doctor looked me square in the eyes and said with a stern voice, 'You can't keep going at that pace. You need to slow down. Otherwise, you won't be here to enjoy the benefits of your hard work.'"

The medical consensus? Trying to "do it all" as a road warrior and working mom had made Alice physically ill. To get back on track, she had to change her concept of what it means to be a good leader and a good parent to her three sons. She finally accepted that it's OK to enlist help at home and to do things like bring the paper plates for the school party and hiring a babysitter who could also help with housework.

Decide to Do Less

Not everyone can afford to pay for help at home, and relationship status and dynamics add complexity to who can share the load around the house. What relief you can get at home is tied to your individual situation and beyond what I can cover here. However, I have talked to far too many women who feel guilty about not doing everything themselves—at home and at work. If that resonates with you, I'd encourage you to be more forgiving of yourself.

"Shoulds" are the tasks or obligations we take on, accompanied by an inner monologue that goes, "I *should* be doing this." But the thought of these tasks gives us no joy. So we do them resentfully or avoid them altogether. As the shoulds pile up, so does the burden of guilt. As a friend once told me, "Stop 'shoulding' all over yourself!"

As you consider the shoulds in your life, don't write another to-do list. Unsubscribe from the idea that you should constantly be doing *more*. Write a "not-to-do" list of all the shoulds you give yourself permission to skip, like inviting the neighbors for dinner and cleaning out the garage. One executive told me, "I will not run or jog unless being chased."

NOT-To-DO LIST
- INViTE NEIGHBORS for DINNER
- CLEAN OUT GARAGE
- RUN/JOG UNLESS CHASED

Alice also had to learn to delegate at work. Even if you don't have direct reports, there are other practical ways to achieve the same end, such as trading tasks with a peer whose strengths complement yours, showing your boss a business case to bring in a contractor or intern, or buying software to automate tasks. And start practicing developmental delegating, or as I like to say, "develegating." Find an up-and-comer in your organization for whom a task maps to the next step in that person's development. Your mentee gets a challenging skill-building assignment, while you get to step up to making a bigger impact. You also get to flex a leadership muscle by serving as a mentor. When you develegate, everybody wins.

In Chapter 6, you'll seek out high-profile stretch opportunities that showcase your leadership brand. It goes without saying that you'll feel stretched by the workload. You'll need help. Alice says it's typical to struggle with letting go of responsibilities, but it doesn't have to be that way. Here are four decisions you can make, right now, to step back with confidence.

Admit You Need to Let Go

As you advance in your career and take ownership of larger projects, it becomes increasingly difficult to juggle additional responsibilities and maintain the quality of your work, "Enlisting support from others is crucial to your own career success," says Alice.

Delegating day-to-day tasks that others can do frees up your time to focus on your most important work—and to contribute in ways that only you can do. It also positions you as a leader who develops people and doesn't micromanage: the opposite of the boss who "kicks down and kisses up."

Invest Time in Delegating

"Delegating takes more time up front," says Alice. There will times when it would be faster to do a task yourself. Don't fall for the immediate gratification of completing small, less consequential tasks when you could be looking to the future to formulate a vision, direction, or strategy.

"In the long run," says Alice, "delegating will save you time and allow you to focus on the bigger picture."

Show People You Believe in Them

If you hoard work that could just as easily be executed by others, it sends a message to others that you think they're not up to the task. Keep this up, and they may start to believe you don't trust them.

"Let your team or your collaborators know you believe in them and that you value their work," says Alice. "Let them know you want them to succeed and grow their careers too." As Alice discovered, trusting and enabling others can be a big challenge, but it is necessary to continue to grow.

Listen to What Inspires People

You might think being an inspirational leader requires being the high-energy human equivalent of a cattle prod. In fact, the opposite can be true. Think of a leader who took the time to listen to you, be fully present, and made you feel like the most important person on the planet, at least for that moment in time. It can be incredibly energizing. One key to Alice's success lies in her love of getting to know the people she works with—what they're capable of, what excites them, their pet peeves, and what they dream of accomplishing. People are motivated to contribute when they see the connection to what inspires them. The best leaders make it their mission to discover what that is, and the only way to find out is to ask questions, listen, and get to know people.

From this point forward, the tasks you let go of can potentially define you more as a leader than what you take on. Underline that. Tattoo it on your brain. Becoming an effective leader begins with taking a step back, and that starts with committing to stepping away, investing in delegating, and believing in others.

> **From this point forward, the tasks you let go of can potentially define you more as a leader than what you take on.**

OWN IT

Shifting from Doing to Delegating

- Create a not-to-do list for your personal life or work life, listing any shoulds you're giving yourself permission to skip—for now or forever.
- Commit to at least one of the following decisions, described above: admit you need to let go, invest time in delegating, show others you believe in them, or listen to what inspires them.
- Think back to the previous Own It exercise where you looked at one month of your calendar. Review the activities you'd like to let go of. Identify any that could go on a not-to-do list.
- Make a list of things to delegate. Choose one that's a priority, and identify the first action to take.

SHIFT 3. OPTIMIZER
TO TRANSFORMER

One reliable way to stand out as a high performer, especially early in your career, is to be an *optimizer*, a person who improves any role, process, or task she or he is handed. The best optimizers are on an unstoppable quest for enhancements, whether developing or streamlining a process, reducing a budget, speeding up execution, or enhancing productivity. But if you want to make a larger impact, stop scouring for incremental improvements and instead go in pursuit of groundbreaking change that can't be undone. When a transformer's work is done, the pickle can't go back to being a cucumber.

Don't think for a moment that you need positional authority to become a wildly successful leader of transformational change either.

It's OK to start small too. The problem you tackle doesn't need to be large, just important.

Early in her career, Leila Pourhashemi was a program manager and consummate optimizer who delivered all of these outcomes, and more. But eventually, her determination to make a bigger impact enticed her to look beyond the bounds of her immediate role and became a force for betterment across an entire organization. Leila, now vice president of business operations with Ancestry, shifted from optimizer to transformer, and you can too.

> **The problem you tackle doesn't need to be large, just important.**

In a role with a previous company, Leila was charged with leading an audacious initiative: to change the way 5,000 employees worked so that they would become more customer focused, so that they, in turn, could transform the way the citizens of the world use money. The results? Within 18 months, there was a 55 percent boost in productivity and a tenfold increase in product releases.

Oh, and there's one more detail you should know. Leila pulled off this tectonic shift with the help of a small team and very little positional power. It all came down to her ability to influence. Here are some keys to her success.

Agree on the Problem

Getting people engaged with a problem they care deeply about and want to solve is one of the most effective ways to influence. But where change initiatives commonly get derailed is in this very first step, says Leila. "What typically happens is that people jump to brainstorming solutions. They take sides and argue about 'my idea' versus 'your idea.' The real issue is that everyone's trying to solve a different problem."

If you can get people to agree on the problem first, instead of defending ownership of their solutions, you can rally around a solution. Along the way, you'll come across people who care about the issue as much as you do.

Enlist Passionate Change Champions

Once the problem and solution were clearly defined, an even bigger challenge emerged: how to get 5,000 people, 100 leaders, and 10 development centers invested in making a change. Says Leila, "It was really important that we reached everybody, but I had a tiny team at the time."

So Leila and her team assembled a volunteer army. They asked for volunteers and were deliberate about finding passionate people across the organization who became 500 change champions. Every champion spoke to least 10 people about what was being done and why.

Flex Your Transformation Muscles

Leila lists five qualities present in those who lead change with influence, not positional power. These five qualities will help you any time you're leading others toward a common goal. But when you're switching from optimizer to transformer, they are crucial:

1. **Conviction:** You have to have conviction in order to influence successfully. "If I don't come across as having conviction that a change will get us to a better place, how will I be able to convince everybody else?" says Leila. Your conviction will help you persist when things get hard, and things *will* get hard.
2. **Passion:** "It's equally as important to be passionate" says Leila. You have to speak with energy and enthusiasm, showing your desire to

help your organization move to a better place. Passion becomes infectious, and people want to join you.

3. **Vision:** "You also have to paint the vision," Leila says. When others see problems, look at how things could be better. A change agent needs to communicate how a change will make employees happier, deliver better products to customers, or make the company more nimble or profitable.

4. **Empathy:** Transformation agents, who are always thinking futuristically, tend to be few steps ahead of everybody else. "You have to meet people where they are," says Leila. You'll need to have empathy, understand where people are today, and map out stepping stones to reach your vision, so people can see where they're going to go.

5. **Relentlessness:** "Not everything you try will work, so you have to keep trying new things until something sticks and the change becomes self-sustaining," says Leila. Until that happens, you have to be relentless and keep trying.

"If you don't feel this way about the change that you want to lead, you should pick a different change as your goal," Leila says. "But when you can bring these five qualities, you'll make a lot of change and you'll have a great career."

OWN IT

Shifting from Optimizer to Transformer

Choose a meaningful business problem that you'd like to see solved:

- Discuss the issue with others. See if you can get them to agree on the core problem, then work together to identify a solution they can rally around.
- While you're having those discussions, look out for people who care about the issue as much as you do. Ask them to be your change champions.
- Identify one step you can take to transform the business problem. Take that step.

- Pick one of the five qualities of those who lead change with influence (conviction, passion, vision, empathy, and being relentless) and start modeling that behavior today.

SHIFT 4. ORDER TAKER TO RULE BREAKER

"You can't leave your career when you're at your height—it will derail you." That was the unwritten rule of career advancement at a company where Holly Meidl worked early in her career. As a rising star in risk consulting for the insurance industry, she was told she would never be able to return to working in a significant role.

When it comes to conventional career wisdom, some rules were meant to be broken. Holly left that company to care for her young family. While being active in her children's schools and the local community, she learned a ton about grassroots leadership and collaborative influence. When Holly reentered the workforce, those lessons helped her leapfrog to a national leadership role at a previous company. Now, vice president of risk services for Ascension, the largest nonprofit healthcare system in the United States, she's living proof that it can pay to break rules.

And let me tell you, some conventional career rules are asking to be broken. See if any of these scenarios sound familiar:

- You must be a senior engineer for three years before becoming a principal engineer.
- You need to meet 75 percent of a role's requirements before applying.
- Only the vice president can renegotiate a deal with a major vendor.
- It's important to pay your dues by doing "grunt work."

I know women who have challenged every one of these so-called rules. Someone said "You can't do that" or "It's never been done before," and they replied, "Watch me!" With courage, good grace, and persistence, they made wildly successful moves.

Taking orders from your boss, doing only what you're told, and never coloring outside the lines of your job description will earn you credit as a good team player, but it won't catapult you further. For that, you need to shift from *order taker* to *rule breaker*.

Being a rule breaker, by its nature, means you have to take risks. To understand which risks to take, let's break risk taking into two subtypes: career risks and business risks.

Career risks: A career risk is an assignment or role that can potentially derail your career. In accepting the risk, you're putting your future on the line. The course of your career depends on your success or failure.

For inspiration, look no further than Allison Unkraut who left an executive position for an entry-level role in a small, unproven company, or Sara Sperling, who took a role for which she had no background or training. Your next career risk could be taking on an international assignment, writing a proposal to expand your role to fit your strengths, or even turning down a promotion that's outside your sweet spot. If you're stuck for ideas, there will be plenty in Chapter 6.

As one sales leader told me, if you're avoiding risks in your career, you might actually be creating *more* risk for yourself. You're not exploiting your full capacity for career growth.

Business risks: Early in your career, the high-stakes bets you place will be weighted more heavily toward career risks. As you advance, the balance shifts in favor of taking more business risks, where your success or failure can have make-or-break consequences for your organization.

Look no further than how Leila Pourhashemi transformed the work practices of 5,000 employees. Other examples of business risks include investing in a new technology, starting up a new division, shaking up a team, turning around a bleeding business unit, making a controversial hire, or discontinuing a product line.

$$\bullet \quad \bullet \quad \bullet$$

In my decades of interviewing highly accomplished women leaders, I've seen how risk taking is necessary as both a career strategy and a business strategy. I've also noticed a universal pattern. Assuming career-related risks early on builds an appetite and tolerance for risk taking that pays off later. That said, it's never too late to start taking more risks. As Nora M.

Denzel, board director with AMD and Ericsson says, "If you don't take risks, you'll always work for someone who does."

Holly Meidl goes so far as to look for examples of risk taking on the résumés of those she interviews and hires. It's a highly prized commodity, in her view, because it shows that an individual is willing to step outside of her or his comfort zone. "In our current global economy," she says, "companies need risk takers and rule breakers."

So, what does it take to be a successful risk taker and rule breaker? I asked Holly how she sizes up the risks associated with a bold career move or business decision. I wanted to understand: How does she know when to conform to the rules, written or unwritten, and when to be creatively disruptive? When do you go all-in?

"Rule breaking is about taking a risk to invest your time, your focus, and even your financial resources to achieve a better outcome," says Holly. It's not a blatant disregard for the "rules" but rather, the intentional act of choosing a path other than the one you've been traveling. It's about doing things differently to find a better way. If you keep a positive attitude, even if you fail, every risk you take brings an opportunity to learn, she says.

Three Rules for Rule Breakers

Holly has three simple rules she learned in school that have continued to guide her. She credits a college professor, Dr. E. J. Leverett, with teaching these risk management principles:

1. Don't risk a lot for a little.
2. Don't risk more than you can afford to lose.
3. Consider the odds or the potential consequences.[3]

"I allow these principles to guide me at times when I am thinking about taking a new risk or breaking a rule," says Holly. Whether you're asking for a promotion outside of the review cycle, reengineering a business process, or even at a blackjack table in Vegas, make these your three rules to live by as you progress from order taker to rule breaker.

OWN IT

Shifting from Order Taker to Rule Breaker

Pick a rule that you'd like to break. Think big. It could involve a career or business risk:

- Apply the three rules of risk management (don't risk a lot for a little, don't risk more than you can afford to lose, and consider the odds or the potential consequences). Decide whether it's worth taking the risk.
- What would be the first step to make this happen? Consider taking it.

SHIFT 5. "ME" TO "WE"

There's one more shift that sums up the whole approach. I like to think of it as the grandmomma of them all: from "me" to "we."

When you're a high performer, enthusiastically stepping up to lead, it's easy to come off as the smartest person in the room. You try to bring the best ideas and set high standards for yourself. No one can doubt your commitment or work ethic. But is this how team performance is unleashed? Not necessarily.

You don't need to be brilliant to bring out the best in everyone around you. You don't need to speak up the most or appear infallible. Instead, be a "force multiplier," someone whose presence in a group is a catalyst for elevating collective performance.

When you shift your attention from your own success to what makes your team or organization successful and train yourself to derive more satisfaction from collective wins than personal ones, you can start to have an impact and influence that reaches beyond your role. This shift in mindset goes to the heart of what it means to be a leader.

When you move your mindset from "me" to "we," everything changes. "If you aspire to lead boldly and courageously, this is the most

> **When you move your mindset from "me" to "we," everything changes.**

powerful shift you can make. There's no doubt about it," says Pamela Stewart, senior vice president of national retail sales with Coca-Cola. I couldn't love her statement more. I completely, wholeheartedly, unequivocally agree.

MAKE SHIFT HAPPEN

Whatever you do, don't build a career around being the ultimate tactician, doer, optimizer, order taker, or problem solver. All of these roles will fade in value relative to the leadership contributions you can make. Stick with them and you'll put a lid on how far you can go and how big a difference you can make. To live up to your brand's promise, you'll need to get your shift together.

I'm not saying this is going to be easy. In fact, it can be far from it. Making the departure from doing to leading can be one of the toughest transitions you'll make in your career, and after reading this chapter, your mind is likely buzzing with all there is to do. You might be sizing yourself up against accomplished confident leaders you know or read about, and you might be worrying about how you'll ever stack up.

Please. Just. Don't.

You're attempting something momentous, new, and difficult, so be kind to yourself. Pick one shift to focus on—the one that makes the most sense for you right now, and concentrate on that new mindset. Catch yourself in the act of thinking the old way, and try to embrace the new way instead. When you feel ready, take a few actions to test out or reinforce the shift. Celebrate every small step as a win, and know that I'm incredibly proud of you.

Here's the list of five key shifts again:

The Shift List

Shift 1. Tactician to strategist

Shift 2. Doing to delegating

Shift 3. Optimizer to transformer

Shift 4. Order taker to rule breaker

Shift 5. "Me" to "we"

In the next exercise, identify which of these transitions will be most crucial to your leadership development in the next year.

OWN IT

Make Shift Happen

Read through The Shift List one more time:

- Which shift will contribute most to your ability to live up to your brand's promise?
- Which shift could derail you, should you fail to make it?
- What's the single most important shift you'll need to work on in the next year?
- How might you catch yourself in the act of thinking the old way, and remind yourself to embrace the new way?
- What actions must you take, or what new behaviors could you take on, to reinforce the shift?

OUTSOURCE IT

Make Shift Happen

This one's for your most leaderly advisors, such as a mentor or manager who has some insight into your leadership development needs as well as what it will take for you to grow and thrive in your organization.

Share your leadership brand statement and The Shift List with her and ask:

- What's the most important shift I should to work on in the next year to deliver on what's promised by my brand statement?
- What actions can I take or what new behaviors could I take on to make the shift?

CHAPTER 5 WRAP-UP

You reimagined your brand. So what?

Your brand is not what you say you are. It's the experience others have when they interact with you. Like it or not, we teach people how to treat us, and your brand is being shaped in every interaction you have. If your head's down, buried in the tactical to-dos, you won't be remembered in a way that's consistent with the leader you aspire to be. So, lift your head up, shift your mindset, and rebalance how you spend your time in favor of more leading, less doing.

This chapter broke down the key shifts in mindset and behavior that will get you there. You can choose to think like a strategist, delegator, transformer, or rule breaker, and stand for making a difference that's bigger than you can accomplish alone.

With actions to match, you can become the embodiment of your brand and show what you're made of. In the next chapter, continue bringing your brand to life by taking on carefully curated roles and assignments that can become career-defining achievements.

6

Go Big or Go Home
Create Career-Defining Moments

> Opportunity does not come gift wrapped.
> You must take risks.
> —**Nina Bhatti,** CEO, Kokko

"I want to bust my guts doing work that's of no consequence whatsoever to my career," said no one, ever. And yet, we've all found ourselves stuck, grinding away at thankless, low-visibility tasks because we wanted to be the overachiever, the good corporate citizen, or felt awkward saying no. You throw up your hand and say, "Sure, I'll do it," then come to regret it.

Sit on that hand for now. I'm going to share an important principle that you need to take full advantage of in order to capitalize on the career-accelerating power that your leadership brand has to offer.

Here it comes . . . wait for it . . .

Work less.

Yes, you read that right. *Work less.* Stick with me here while I explain what that means. Please, don't go and dump your unfinished business onto your boss's desk and say, "Jo Miller told me I should work less. It's 2 p.m. *Hasta la vista*, sister." If you do that, you'll make us both quite unpopular. Don't put down this book without reading the next paragraph.

Here's what "work less" means in the context of building your brand as a woman of influence. One reliable way to torpedo your future leadership prospects is to be the heroine who tries to do it all. If you're a hard worker who develops a reputation for hard work, what do you attract more of? More work. Think about it: if you're the one who is always saying yes to the little things, the time-consuming busywork, and messy tactical to-dos, that will eventually become your brand. You'll keep attracting more of the same.

We also need to talk about "office housework," because women and minorities are doing more of it.[1]

What's office housework? Some is actual workplace housekeeping, like tidying up the break room or rearranging chairs around a conference table. The term also encompasses communal tasks like having lunch catered, setting up an offsite, or giving a new colleague a tour of the photocopier and restrooms. By definition, office housework is unseen and unrewarded. No one sealed a promotion to senior director on the strength of being awesome at corralling conference-call RSVPs or the "just-in-time" replacement of coffee filters. I'm not saying you should never contribute to office housework. Instead, take a stand for sharing the load equitably. Don't let your leadership strengths and brand get buried under a mountain of low-level, inconsequential tasks.

Successful leaders don't do it all. They don't even try. Here's what they do instead:

- Former "ultimate tactician" Dona Munsch analyzes her calendar for trends that help her reallocate her time from tactical activities to more strategic ones.
- High-tech sales executive Alice Katwan trusts her direct reports to handle day-to-day team management.
- Transformational change leader Leila Pourhashemi enlists support from volunteer champions to drive wide-scale change.
- One sales executive told me when an email comes in with a nonurgent request, she'll let it cool off in her inbox for 48 hours. Minor issues frequently get resolved without her lifting a finger.

Want more ideas? Talk to a mentor about how she or he deflects the minutiae of everyday work life in order to lock focus on the bigger picture.

Working less on low-prestige busywork is only half of this chapter's core message. This part's just as important:

Work hard on the *right* opportunities.

MISSTEP 7

Accepting low-visibility assignments is Misstep 7, and the remedy is making good choices. You won't always get to choose what you work on, but when you do have a say, sidestep busywork, tactical to-dos, and incremental optimizing.

Make the Leaderly Move of *creating career-defining moments* by devoting yourself instead to wholeheartedly crushing it at the tasks, projects, assignments, and roles that put your leadership brand front and center. Do more than show up. Make an outsized contribution. Give the best of your time and energy to the opportunities where you can be a difference maker, practice the leadership mindsets and behaviors you outlined in Chapter 5, and do work that's wet-your-pants exciting.

In this chapter, you'll get clear on what a true career-defining opportunity looks like and develop a checklist of criteria so you'll recognize one when you see one. You'll also learn how to respond when you're asked to work on something that's *not* career enhancing.

We'll talk about strategies to locate opportunities that fit within the leadership niche you identified in Chapter 3 and showcase the leadership brand you defined in Chapter 4. And don't miss the tips on how to make the most of any big break by delivering like a rock star.

DEVELOP YOUR COURAGE MUSCLE

Nithya Ruff was feeling nervous but excited. The general manager of a major division of her company had come to her with an unexpected proposal: Would she like to lead his entire product management team? It was a large group, responsible for a significant piece of business, worth over $300 million in revenue.

Nithya, now head of Comcast's Open Source Program Office, knew it was a critical role, but she'd never been responsible for anything this big before. Still, she reminded herself, there was a reason why her GM was asking her to take the job. "He believed in me, and so I needed to believe in myself too and see what he saw in me," says Nithya.

So while she was new to managing such a large team, Nithya weighed the benefits of the expanded responsibility and took in the magnitude of opportunity. She accepted the role, and out of that first budding act of leadership courage, her career blossomed. Years later, looking back on that experience, Nithya says, "Truly, I learned how to grow. I learned how to be uncomfortable. While I certainly had my struggles in the role, I learned how to build a strong organization, delegate more, and build strategic relationships."

If you're not pushing the limits of your comfort zone—by raising your hand for an assignment that's a stretch or a challenging new role— you're not exploiting the full capacity of your leadership potential.

Still, there's a psychological mind trick we play on ourselves, known as *negativity bias*, where we tend to overestimate risk and underestimate opportunity. As Margie Warrell, author of *Brave* has pointed out, we tend to overestimate the probability of something going wrong, underestimate our ability to handle the consequences of risk, and discount or deny the cost of inaction. For all of these reasons, we often end up sticking with the status quo.[2]

> **If you're not pushing the limits of your comfort zone—by raising your hand for an assignment that's a stretch or a challenging new role—you're not exploiting the full capacity of your leadership potential.**

At any stage of your career, it's easier (though not necessarily safer) to stay comfortable. Every time you take a new risk, your risk tolerance grows, and you'll enhance your readiness to take on the next new challenge. "It is so important to not play it safe if you want to lead, grow, and get noticed," says Nithya. "Courage—like a muscle—is developed with practice," says Nithya. "So start taking small risks. And, soon, you'll find that your courage is well developed."

AN UNMET NEED

One year into her first job as a junior software engineer, Nina Bhatti had done well at developing her first product. As a thank-you, she was invited to attend her company's annual sales meeting. "I noticed that everyone was very grumpy about one feature of our device," says Nina, who is now CEO of Kokko. The product sold for up to a quarter of a million dollars, but it had no way to print the data that it was capturing. Although the feature was scheduled to be added in 18 months, the sales team was moping about lost sales due to the lack of printing support.

Nina thought to herself, "This is an unmet need. A lot of people would really care if we fixed it." She studied the product's architecture and devised an innovative solution that could be delivered in three months. When she mentioned it to her senior engineer colleagues, they got excited. After getting buy-in from executives, Nina got to lead the project—her first business leadership role.

As a result, Nina was little more than one year into her career when her solution became "the big reveal" at the next companywide sales meeting. Nina earned a promotion and greater visibility, and in an outcome that was even more meaningful to her, she helped her organization exceed its financial goals. There was a big difference, Nina points out, between waiting for an assignment versus spotting a problem and taking the initiative to fix it.

Nithya's and Nina's stories are representative of a pattern. Over the past two decades I have coached and interviewed countless leaders who have had remarkable career success, one thing is abundantly clear: *they did not get to where they are by playing it safe.* Most were able to look back to an instance when they put their reputation on the line by tackling a challenging problem, project, or post. The risk of failure was very real. They took the leap anyway, delivered results, and made a difference. For many, like Nithya and Nina, the accomplishment became a defining moment in their career.

THE CAREER-PROPELLING POWER OF
STRETCH OPPORTUNITIES

Want to uncover a bigger, bolder vision for your career than you can imagine today? Try taking on a stretch opportunity: a task, project, assignment, or role that breaks with what you're historically known for. To effectively deliver, you will be required to sharpen your professional, business, and/or leadership skills. Do well and you'll reinvent how your organization sees you—and how you see yourself.

These career-defining scenarios fall into two categories: stretch roles and stretch assignments.[3]

A stretch assignment requires you to temporarily step beyond the responsibilities of your day job to take on a challenging new task or project. Stretch assignments can be assigned to you, like the time Cindy Pace was asked to take over planning a large conference. Or you can self-initiate, like the time Nina Bhatti took the initiative to respond to an unmet customer need.

A stretch role is a challenging new permanent role that requires you to make a larger impact, expand your scope of responsibility, and learn new skills or ways of thinking. As an example, look no further than Nithya Ruff, or Sara Sperling being invited to set up her company's diversity and inclusion function from scratch, with no prior experience in that area.

Going forward, you'll find that I'll frequently bundle stretch assignments and stretch roles together and refer to them as "stretch opportunities" or "stretches." These are highly visible, and they can make your skills, value, and work ethic known beyond your immediate work group. They can offer exposure to a wider network of peer-level collaborators, experts, stakeholders, and senior-level leaders. At the same time, you can demonstrate your commitment to your organization's goals and make a bulked-up contribution to them.

Nina Simosko's path to becoming CEO of NTT Innovation Institute Inc. was paved with both types of stretches. No matter what stage of your career, saying yes to high-visibility opportunities should be at the top of your list of priorities, she says. "For those starting out, it indicates willingness and motivation, and it helps mark you out as a future leader." Taking on challenging assignments early in your career also builds an affinity for leadership and tolerance for risk taking that can pay off in the long run—but it's never too late to start. Says Nina, "For midcareer leaders, taking on high-visibility projects can accelerate your progression, open up additional responsibilities and opportunities, and signal your interest for executive leadership roles."

The stakes can be high, but there's evidence by the bucketload that says a well-executed stretch can propel you to new heights.

Stretch opportunities are fuel for advancement. According to a Catalyst report, 40 percent of women in leadership positions say that taking "difficult, visible" assignments was key to their advancement.[4]

They're an accelerant for skills development. When one survey asked more than 800 international executives what had helped them unleash their potential, 71 percent cited stretch assignments—and no other form of career development came close.[5] Stretch or rotational assignments are the hands-down most valuable leadership development activity, ahead of training, mentoring, building relationships, 360-degree assessments, and exposure to senior leaders.[6]

The extra compensation doesn't hurt, either. People who land stretch assignments are also more likely to get raises.[7]

Here's the catch, though:

Women are less likely to attract stretch opportunities. While these high-profile, visible projects and mission-critical roles are a proven key to advancing further, faster, women attract fewer of these crucial experiences.[8] Which is all the more reason to advocate for your access to these career-defining experiences or devise your own.

In her book *Lean In: Women, Work, and the Will to Lead*, Sheryl Sandberg shared an intriguing statistic: "An internal report at Hewlett-Packard revealed that women only apply for open jobs if they think they meet 100 percent of the criteria listed." Men, Sandberg wrote, will apply when they believe they meet 60 percent of the requirements. Though a somewhat mysterious source was cited, this factoid took on an appealing truthlike quality, and it has been widely quoted in articles, books, and diversity programs as one reason why women are advancing less rapidly. Ouch.

To find out why women attract fewer stretch opportunities, Selena Rezvani, vice president of consulting and research at Be Leaderly, and I coauthored a study that examined this question: Do women and men differ in how they assess their readiness to step up to a challenging new assignment or role? Be Leaderly surveyed 1,500 US professionals, and we published the results and analysis in the report *Out of the Comfort Zone: How Women and Men Size up Stretch Assignments—and Why Leaders Should Care.*

One of our key findings was that in order to apply for a job, women felt that they needed to meet, on average, 75 percent of the qualifications listed for the role. The answer from men was exactly the same, 75 percent. We're proud to have busted that myth.

There was one further dimension to this puzzle though. We also found that when women assess how ready they are for a challenging new role or assignment, they're more likely than men to underestimate, or "round down," their skills, and they are less likely to overestimate, or "round up," what they know or can do. One reason could be that we're less likely than men to receive specific, actionable performance feedback,[9] despite asking for it no less frequently.[10]

If you tend to understate or downplay your qualifications, here are some suggestions for assessing your readiness to stretch:

- Keep asking for feedback. If your request is dismissed, be persistent.
- As procurement leader Karen Stuckey urged in Chapter 2, keep developing a strong internal compass for insightful, accurate self-evaluation.
- Dial up the chutzpah, set modesty aside, and give yourself and your skills the benefit of doubt.

OWN IT

Your Next Stretch

Think about whether the next big career opportunity you go after will be a stretch role or a stretch assignment.

THE IDEAL STRETCH RATIO

The ideal stretch should challenge you without defeating you, and it should draw you out of your comfort zone yet fall short of pushing you too far too soon. Overcommit, and you not only risk burnout but also lost credibility. Beware too of staying so safe and comfortable that you fall into a rut and become stagnant or disengaged.

To avoid overstretching or understretching, Tara Jaye Frank of TJF Career Modeling recommends sticking to the following rule: "Embrace a stretch opportunity that's about 70 percent what you know and do well and that's aligned with your experiences, your talents, and your passions." The remaining 30 percent should be the caliber of challenge that makes you wonder, "What the heck am I doing?" That way, you can achieve the benefits of a stretch without compromising yourself, your work, or your team, explains Tara Jaye.

You might be wondering: "But what if I stretch, mess up, and fail?" Failures are your hard-won lessons, and they add to your credibility. In Chapter 7, I'll show you how to make them part of your brand's story and share your hard-earned knowledge.

Risks of Overstretching
- Burnout
- Lost credibility

- Compromised work quality
- Missing your deliverables
- Making others pick up the slack

Risks of Understretching
- Being underutilized
- Remaining a "doer"
- Falling back on existing skills
- Playing it safe
- Becoming bored or disengaged

OWN IT

The Ideal Stretch Ratio

- Evaluate whether you're overstretching or understretching in your current work.
- If you're doing either, look at what, if anything, would need to change for you to achieve the right amount of stretch (70 percent what you know and do well, and 30 percent "What the heck am I doing?"). Decide on your first step and take action.

CRITERIA FOR A CAREER-DEFINING OPPORTUNITY

Now that you know your leadership brand, seek out stretches that fulfill your brand's promise. To help identify opportunities, look for ways you can directly support your organization's strategic plan and goals. Use that knowledge to land plum assignments that allow you to demonstrate your ability to deliver results. The resulting visibility will heighten your value and strengthen your brand.

As wonderful as stretches can be, remember that they need to be the right ones for you. So no matter how enticing a new opportunity sounds, and no matter how persuasive the person offering it to you might be, *don't immediately say yes.* Gather as many details as possible, and say you'd like time to think about it and make the best decision for yourself and the organization. Defer your acceptance until you've assessed whether the assignment will be a career-defining one.

Use the checklist below any time you're considering taking on a high-profile project, stretch assignment, or new position. It will help you put your guardrails in place and make a great choice:

- ☐ Does this opportunity reinforce the leadership brand you want to be known for?
- ☐ Does this opportunity allow you to deliver valuable results to your organization?

Saying yes to those two questions is essential to your ongoing success. If an assignment doesn't align with and support the leadership brand you're out to build or it doesn't allow you to deliver a win to your organization, it's unlikely to add a lot of value to your career. But if the assignment includes these two elements, plus at least two of the following seven supporting criteria in the checklist below, get ready to go out and smash it:

- ☐ Move you forward on your chosen career trajectory
- ☐ Help you develop new skills and business acumen
- ☐ Provide you with your ideal amount of stretch
- ☐ Give you the influence you need to succeed, along with adequate support from your management
- ☐ Make your value visible to your organization's leaders
- ☐ Meaningfully expand your network
- ☐ Connect you to potential sponsors

You can get both of these checklists at www.jomiller.com/stretch.

So before volunteering for or saying yes to a significant new project or role, make sure it will achieve your ideal stretch ratio, while adding some shiny new bullet points to your résumé. Be prepared to be ruthless—but diplomatic—about negotiating and landing assignments that meet your criteria. Choose your next opportunity well, and it might become a defining moment for you. Pick a succession of stretches well, and you'll have a truly remarkable career.

OWN IT

Criteria for a Career-Defining Opportunity

- Customize the checklist of criteria for a career-defining opportunity, and add any other decision criteria that are important to you.
- Keep your checklist handy so you can use it whenever you're sizing up a stretch opportunity.
- Review the top three priorities you're working on right now. Do any meet the criteria for a career-defining opportunity? If not, can you upgrade one to be career defining—for example, by negotiating with your boss to be the one to give presentations to your leadership team or asking for an extended deadline so you can go after a more challenging target?

BRAND BUILDERS VERSUS BRAND BUSTERS

But let's get real for a moment: not all stretch opportunities are created equal. Some are great for building your reputation, while others will only bury it.

Collins Aerospace business leader Chris Turkovich had recently earned his MBA and was looking for ways to build a new reputation as a strategic thinker when he was invited to take on a stretch assignment to develop a business plan for a low-cost product to break into a new market. He weighed the probability of being successful against the added workload and saw a no-win scenario, so he politely declined to participate.

Later that year, he noticed that his business unit lacked a single point of contact for coordinating requests for investments in new product development. Where the previous assignment would have recycled his existing skills, filling this yet unrecognized, unmet need would require him to develop new strengths, including strategic thinking and influencing stakeholders across the organization. He offered to take this on, won approval from his leadership, and shouldered the additional workload for the month it took to complete the assignment. As predicted, it paid off. Chris explained, "I built credibility as a strategic leader, which helped me land the role that I'm in today where I manage and develop other program managers."

Again, aim for high-profile projects, roles, and assignments that stretch you without overwhelming you, so you can deliver a consistently high caliber of work.

Want more specifics? Here are four types of situations to steer clear of:

- **Brand burier:** A low-visibility assignment or intractable problem that requires you to work ungodly hours without obvious benefits.
- **"Craptastic" detour:** An assignment that's super high profile but spotlights the opposite of what you want to be known for, diluting your brand or knocking you off your intended career path.
- **Stretching too thin:** You may have heard the motivational mantra, "Bite off more than you can chew, and chew like hell." This is less inspiring when you're already chomping like crazy to get through your existing workload and you're at risk of burning out.
- **Right assignment, wrong time:** A great opportunity can hit at the wrong time when other priorities in life take precedence. Give yourself permission to declare a stretch-free phase.

One more caveat: It's good to commit to stretches at a cadence that builds in some recovery time. Allow yourself to stretch, recover, repeat.

As Dumbledore once said to Harry Potter, "It is our choices, Harry, that show what we truly are, far more than our abilities."[11]

> It's good to commit to stretches at a cadence that builds in recovery time. Allow yourself to stretch, recover, repeat.

ARTFULLY SAYING NO

When you're invited to work on something that you're truly, innately in-spired to take on, it's easy to say yes. Other times, your gut or your check-list tell you to it's a no. And the assignments you say no to can be as career defining as the ones you accept.

Knowing that, the way you turn down an ill-fitting opportunity can do a lot to increase your chances of attracting a better match next time too. I spoke to Coca-Cola retail sales leader Pamela Stewart about how to artfully decline.

If you feel that opportunities are scarce or that this is a one-time only offer, you'll only ever say yes, and that can be a problem, Pamela points out. "To high achievers, who are often people pleasers, the idea of saying no can be painful, but the inability to set boundaries around your time and space erodes the opportunity to attack your boldest dreams," says Pamela. It's her belief that it's important to decline any opportunity that you know is going to infringe on time with your family, a career bound-ary, your thinking space, or time to rejuvenate. "You'll show up a better person and a stronger leader," says Pamela.

To diplomatically say no, Pamela recommends expressing your grati-tude and providing some context. For example, you could say:

"I'm grateful to be considered for this opportunity. But, based on my schedule and other demands, I'm unable to help in this instance."

Then move on, *guilt free.*

One of Pamela's hard-won career lessons is how much more guilt she would feel about overcommitting and encroaching on family time.

If you're still feeling uncomfortable about saying no, dig deep and try to understand the source. If you're wired to please others, or if pushing back feels politically unwise, it's worth thinking through why.

When you decline a stretch because it falls outside your career road-map or the scope of your brand, it doesn't need to hurt the relationship or be the end of the conversation. Here are some additional scripts to educate others about what you'd be excited to contribute.

After politely declining, you can add: "Please keep me in mind for [name your ideal assignment]."

One way to both deflect the offer and promote yourself as a leader is to help others stretch: "This is outside of my expertise as a [describe your leadership brand]. Have you considered asking [name a colleague]? It could be a great opportunity for her."

If you accept but also want to stretch in a different way, you can say: "I'd be happy to help out, and I can actually do more. Please also consider me for [name your ideal assignment]."

FINDING YOUR NEXT
CAREER-DEFINING OPPORTUNITY

Some people seem to have all the career luck. They land the groundbreaking, career-making assignments, and the best jobs seem to find *them*. How do they do it? Here's a hint: often, the best opportunities are right in front of you, hiding in plain sight.

Angie Hemmelgarn already held a demanding HR leadership role when her previous company formed a new business unit that needed a human resources business partner.

"We were having a global restructuring meeting, and I heard about a new group that was being formed to address product quality issues. The CEO wanted to put more focus on this group," says Angie, now chief human resources officer with Claritas. "I got excited about the fact that this was new and different. I had never worked with operations, engineering, or technology groups before, and I wanted to help out. I pulled my manager aside and said, 'I'm really excited about this. I want this opportunity. Do you think that this is something I could do?'"

Angie volunteered to take on the extra workload in addition to her day-to-day role and won her manager's approval. The new business unit got its HR partner, and Angie built knowledge and relationships that set her up for success in subsequent roles. It was a classic example of how a great stretch assignment can bolster a career: Everybody wins.

As you scan your environment, keep your checklist in mind, so you can tune out the noise and pick up on career-defining opportunities. Here are five places to look for opportunities to showcase your brand and your value.

Opportunity 1. What's Already on Your Plate?

Before volunteering for a high-profile assignment or proposing a new project from scratch, examine more closely what's already on your plate. It's quite possible that something you're already working on could lead to your next big career-defining opportunity.

Scrutinize your current workload to see if there's anything that both aligns with your leadership brand and would enable you to deliver a win to your organization. If so, this could be a career-defining opportunity. Go all-in to elevate it from just another to-do-list item to your top priority.

Opportunity 2: Do the Hard Thing

"Take the job no one wants" is advice that's often given to aspiring leaders. I've interviewed numerous leaders who advanced by always being the one to take the hardest roles and solve the toughest problems.

Kimberly Scardino, senior vice president of finance with The Home Depot is one of them. "I would seek out pain points or areas of unaddressed need and work to solve them. Someone who finds ways to solve hard problems and bring folks together will often emerge as a leader," she says.

But you'll need to avoid the trap of investing the best of your energy in an intractable, thankless, low-visibility task. Armed with the checklist of criteria for a career-defining opportunity, you'll know when to stop playing it safe and volunteer to do the hard thing.

Opportunity 3. Lighten a Leader's Load

Always keep in mind the perspectives, needs, and objectives of people a level or two below you and a level or two above you, says Kimberly. She made her mark early on in an accounting department by noticing areas that needed attention but management didn't have time to address. These included recruiting and staffing, which she stepped in to lead. Administrative and entry-level staff began looking to her for her leadership. Kimberly came to know them well. As her career progressed, she invited the most talented to join her teams, and together they became wildly successful.

Her advice to budding leaders is to pay attention to the leadership responsibilities your management doesn't have time for, especially ones that would be a step up in responsibility for you.

Opportunity 4. Fill a Gap

Every business has important tasks that are falling through the cracks because they're not part of anyone's job description. Look closely and you'll notice the gaps: inefficient processes, underperforming projects, unmet customer needs, and leaderless teams. The seasoned leaders I've interviewed aren't comfortable with the status quo. They are relentless gap spotters. Want examples? I've included a few at www.jomiller.com/fillagap to inspire you.

Pay attention to what people routinely complain about, or when they say, "We've always done it this way" or "Someone really ought to fix this." Keep your antennae up, and when you spot a gap, ask yourself, "Could I be the one to fill it?"

Opportunity 5. Simply Ask

Finally, don't underestimate the power of speaking up. Take a risk and raise your hand for the role or project you covet. Educate, and reeducate, your leaders about what you'd like to get involved with.

As HR leader Angie Hemmelgarn says, "Be bold. Push yourself. And get comfortable being uncomfortable."

OWN IT

Find Your Next Career-Defining Opportunity

Investigate the following options to see if your next groundbreaking, career-making assignment is hiding in plain sight:

- What's already on your plate?
- Do the hard thing.
- Lighten a leader's load.
- Fill a gap.
- Simply ask.

OUTSOURCE IT

Find Your Next Career-Defining Opportunity

Let your management and mentors know what you're looking for in your next stretch opportunity. Ask them to keep an eye out for you.

EXECUTE YOUR ASSIGNMENT LIKE A ROCK STAR

When you're entrusted with a high-profile opportunity, delivering results brings instant credibility and exposure. You're going to be watched and evaluated, so get ready to go forth and slay. Do well, and you'll kick open doors to future opportunities.

When Tara Jaye Frank was vice president of consumer platforms at Hallmark Cards, her manager asked her to take on a stretch assignment in addition to her line management role.

> You're going to be watched and evaluated, so get ready to go forth and slay. Do well, and you'll kick open doors to future opportunities.

It was to serve as an advocate to help the company think differently in its approach to multicultural consumers. When she evaluated the many different models that other companies were using, one stood out: a multicultural center of excellence. Tara Jaye took the idea to her boss, who asked to see a detailed proposal for how such a center might enhance Hallmark's business.

Excited by the proposal and its potential, Tara Jaye created a charter with short- and long-term goals to embed multicultural insights across the entire enterprise and translate those insights into bold business opportunities. What started out as a well-executed side project ultimately led Tara Jaye to envision, establish, and lead the center in a new role as vice president of multicultural strategy.

Inspired by Tara Jaye and leaders like her, here are some keys to success for executing a career-defining stretch like a rock star.[12]

Rock Star Move 1. Bring a Beginner's Mindset

When we tackle something new, many of us rush to convince everyone that we know exactly what we're doing. So when we have questions or we're unsure about how something works, we keep it to ourselves. We go it alone and try to figure it out. Whatever you do, don't do that or you'll deny yourself the opportunity be a beginner, to learn, and to soak up knowledge.

Don't underestimate how your beginner's mindset, raw enthusiasm, and fresh set of eyes can be reinvigorating to experienced players who may have gotten so close to the work that they're no longer seeing what's possible. As gender equality executive Shuchi Sharma likes to say, "Just because you're inexperienced doesn't mean you're inept."

Rock Star Move 2. Be Inquisitive

Be as inquisitive as you can possibly be. Open yourself up to new perspectives by speaking to a wide cross-section of people involved.

Ask executives why they felt it was important for you to devote time to this issue and what a successful execution of this assignment would look like to them. Also, speak with colleagues and stakeholders on the project to identify shared goals and challenges you may encounter. Speak to people who have done this type of work before or experienced its impact as a customer.

When you find others who care about your cause, strengthen ties with them. Enlist them into your volunteer support squad for help with problem solving, influencing, and advocacy.

Rock Star Move 3. Overdeliver

You can't overdeliver on an unclear objective, so invest time up front to get clear on your goals. Have conversations with your management to clarify what "great" looks like, and give yourself time to think and strategize. Document where you're starting from, so you can measure progress, give updates along the way, and highlight the results when you're done.

And don't lose sight of the opportunity that's been entrusted to you. If you're selected for a highly visible assignment, it means someone took a risk on your behalf and put her reputation on the line to advocate for you. This person, along with your organization, is invested in your success and will be watching to see how you perform. Someone staked their belief in you. Don't let that person down by giving anything less than all you've got.

Rock Star Move 4. Utilize the Springboard

Career-defining roles and assignments can become important stepping stones on the way to your next big career milestone, so begin with the end in mind, and be clear on what you hope to gain. Whether it is to develop new technical or leadership skills, strengthen relationships with colleagues and influencers, develop a certain leadership style or brand, or assure your organization that you're ready for the next role, keep your lofty career goal firmly in mind as you execute on the assignment.

"I always look at stretch assignments as springboard opportunities," says Tara Jaye. "Use this moment to your fullest advantage. You can go on to do bigger and better things, meet more people, broaden your network, and expand your knowledge base. Take this opportunity and do amazing things with it."

OWN IT

Execute Your Assignment Like a Rock Star

If you're working on a career-defining stretch, use these keys to success to make sure you're crushing it:

- Bring a beginner's mindset.
- Be inquisitive.
- Overdeliver.
- Utilize the springboard.

CHAPTER 6 WRAP-UP

Assignments and roles that achieve the ideal amount of stretch can be career transforming, and they aren't all that scarce if you know where to look. In this chapter, you developed a checklist of what to look for in assignments to wholeheartedly go after, and you learned to diplomatically step aside from opportunities where you can't showcase your brand or add value. Choose your stretches carefully, and execute them like a star, and you'll have an incredible career.

Next, in Chapter 7, you'll ensure that your work gets the exposure it deserves—even when (not if) you occasionally mess up and fail.

Amplify Your Accomplishments
Don't Be the Best-Kept Secret

> It's not what you know, and it's not who you know.
> It's who knows what you know.
> —**Nora M. Denzel,**
> board director, AMD and Ericsson

Do you remember the first time at work you accomplished something you were really proud of and it was met with appreciation?

I do. I glowed when I heard that a project I'd suggested and then ran with (digitizing some financial records) was praised by the firm's partners. It also earned me a significant bump in salary, so I made a mental bookmark: "Keep doing what I just did." I put my head down and continued to work hard, assuming that I would continue to be singled out for the quality of what I produced.

And that's where I got stuck.

Turns out, great performance is not the standalone foundation for sustained career momentum we'd all like to believe it is.

As leader of a large organization that helps provide over 4 billion meals a year to people facing hunger, one of the key things Feeding America CEO Claire Babineaux-Fontenot continues to try to understand is who is in her talent pool and what their strengths are. "I have to make decisions about the direction of our organization," says Claire. If an employee has not made clear what his or her specific skill set is, that individual can miss out on tailor-made golden opportunities, she says. Meanwhile, the organization and those it serves miss out on the opportunity to benefit from the person's talents.

"In the name of modesty, we sometimes hide our talents, creating missed opportunities for our organizations and for ourselves," says Claire. Know what your unique talents are, she urges, and expose and leverage them in service to your organization. There's nothing untoward about being honest about what you do well. "Your company cannot fully appreciate how to leverage you as a resource if the company does not have visibility into what your unique talents are. So, don't deny your company that chance," she says.

Are the people you work with aware of all that you have to offer?

Take a moment to appreciate how easy it is for them to misinterpret something as intangible as your leadership brand. By making your voice heard, your brand known, and your value visible, you'll make life better and easier for everyone (yourself included).

Remember, if you're a hard worker who develops a reputation for hard work, you can expect to attract more work and not necessarily the recognition that's no doubt well deserved. We Australians describe someone with her nose to the grindstone as "head down, tail up." Visualize how that looks. Which part of you is most visible? Possibly not your best . . . asset.

Your work doesn't speak for itself.

This chapter will help you make your leadership brand, value, and accomplishments visible—in a style that's authentically yours. As Fran Berman, Hamilton Distinguished Professor in Computer Science at Rensselaer Polytechnic Institute, says, "Don't wait for the recognition fairy."

FINDING YOUR VOICE

To have an influential voice and be a leader who makes an impact, let alone get credit for your track record and get people to see your potential, *don't be the best-kept secret in your organization.* This is one of my favorite mantras.

When Stephanie Matthews worked as a producer in broadcast news, promoting her expertise and accomplishments was something of a non-issue. Her television shows, stories, and writing were highly visible thanks to the nature of her work. But after making a career change into public relations, she discovered a new reality: she needed to step up and make her voice heard, own her ideas, and do personal PR to build her leadership brand.

"I had to learn how to speak for myself and become an advocate for myself and for my team," says Stephanie, now executive director at the PR agency Golin. "It's not enough to find your voice. You've also got to use your voice," she says.

Stephanie, who has worked on public relations for household name brands, says building your own leadership brand requires bragging about yourself in a tactful way and calling attention to the great work that you're doing. Stephanie found that hard at first. Here are four strategies she developed:

- **Don't wait for your annual review.** Stephanie started simply, scheduling weekly check-ins with her boss with the point of getting him up to speed on what was happening. The idea is to create a casual cadence for sharing accomplishments, rather than saving everything up for a performance review.
- **Double down on wins.** A constructive way to show what you know is to take what you worked on in one area and reproduce those best practices in another area, says Stephanie. The bigger the business impact, the better. "Being able to tie accomplishments to bottom-line growth is an easy way to brag about yourself—without seeming boastful," she says.

> The idea is to create a casual cadence for sharing accomplishments, rather than saving everything up for a performance review.

- **Know what differentiates you.** "My passion is the intersection of social media and news media," says Stephanie. "That's where I thrive. I'm a news junkie and obsessed with the way we're getting our news." Identifying your passion, deepening your knowledge in that area, and pouncing on opportunities to share your expertise will put you well on your way to becoming a sought-after voice of authority in your industry. Says Stephanie, "Understanding what differentiates you is a key to unlocking new opportunities both internally and externally."

- **Connect, and share your expertise.** Stephanie's specialization in integrated media made her a global resource across her agency, which in turn connected her to teams with different, and often complementary, areas of expertise she would not have otherwise met. "Being exposed to other people's smart ideas is the biggest benefit you'll receive from using your voice," says Stephanie.

THE STRUGGLE IS REAL

When 240 senior leaders of a Silicon Valley tech company were asked to name the factors that got them promoted to their level, one eclipsed all others, and it wasn't professional expertise, delivering business results, or leadership skills. *Visibility* was the most important factor in their advancement.[1] Researchers Shelley Correll and Lori Mackenzie defined *visibility* as "a complex interaction of perceived skills (particularly technical and leadership ones), access to stretch assignments, and being known—and liked—by influential senior leaders within informal networks." All three components—skills, stretches, and sponsors—are necessary to advance.

Another study found that women who were the most proactive in making their achievements visible advanced further, had greater career satisfaction, and were more likely to attract sponsors. And making achievements known was the *only* career advancement strategy associated with pay increases.[2]

So why is visibility so hard to get right?

Of 1,200 workshop participants I surveyed, almost all women, 90 percent felt their work was a valuable contribution to their organization's success (naturally, because who wouldn't?), but 60 percent were not actively taking steps to make people aware of their accomplishments. And it wasn't for lack of desire.

Having their value and contributions recognized was *the number 1 most common challenge* the workshop participants cited. Hands down, end of story. Here's how some described their discomfort:

- I'm a go-getter and hardworking individual, but I struggle with marketing myself to the right people the right way.
- I've received feedback that not enough other managers know what I do. I'm great at branding and promoting others, but have a hard time doing it for myself.
- The people around me who get promoted are self-advocates who push their agenda. I can't see myself doing that.

Many more wrote comments like those. The palpable frustration made my heart ache.

On the other hand, we've all worked with people who, to put it mildly, overdid the self-promotion. They hog the limelight, inflate their contributions, claim others' work as their own, and divert attention away from the people who make real, substantive contributions. But the gravest injustice of all this? They create the impression that it's sleazy to celebrate your own excellence and achievements.

So it's understandable if you decided "I never want to be like that" and stopped drawing attention to your work. Finding the right, balanced approach can be confusing as heck. Let's look at what the real objective really is, because it's *not* self-promotion.

If you want to be seen as an A player:

Amplify the Accomplishments that Align with your Aspirations.

MISSTEP 8

If you've been *downplaying your accomplishments*, which is Misstep 8, take note: the Leaderly Move to make instead is *amplifying the accomplishments that align with your aspirations*. Don't just tattoo this one on your brain. Encourage your colleagues to get matching tattoos too.

To be clear: The objective is *not* to indiscriminately promote yourself, or grab a bullhorn and overshare. The goal is to amplify the accomplishments that are most aligned with where you aspire to go. Say it with me one more time: *Amplify the accomplishments that align with my aspirations*.

THREE RULES OF THUMB FOR AMPLIFYING ACCOMPLISHMENTS

You've seen what can happen when self-promotion goes awry, but have you ever stopped to analyze why that happens?

I've given this some thought, so let's break down three rules of thumb for appropriately, effectively amplifying your accomplishments.

Rule 1. Go for Undiluted Greatness

Listing more accomplishments is not necessarily better, due to a phenomenon called the "Presenter's Paradox."

Say you built an algorithm that reduced customer wait times by one-third, and you're excited to update your boss. It can't hurt to also mention that you helped pick out the new color scheme for the break room . . . right?

This is an example of how our instincts about selling ourselves can be surprisingly off, says Heidi Grant of the Neuroleadership Institute. "Highly favorable or positive attributes get diminished in the eye of the beholder when they are presented in the company of only moderately favorable or positive attributes," says Heidi. Your overall perceived value actually *decreases* when you throw in items of lesser quality. Think of it as lowering your average. So the next time you're reporting what you're working on, mention your *highest-value activities* that best reflect your brand and then *stop talking*.

Rule 2. Stay Authentically on Brand

If you try to promote accomplishments in a way that's mismatched with the way you lead and communicate, it can come off as forced or inauthentic— and diminish your brand.

Let's say your brand is "leader who develops other leaders." Talking up how you automated an administrative task is not bad, per se, but it could undermine the brand perception you're out to build. A better method would be to call out examples of leadership shown by your team (and invite your boss to a meeting to hand out awards.)

But if your brand *is* all about "calming the chaos," and you're an unstoppable force for eliminating tedious admin tasks that keep people from getting real work done, then talk that up with everything you've got, and create a presentation about it. And don't just deliver it once. Share your knowledge and best practices with multiple teams, blog about them, and teach a webinar.

To set yourself up for success, find some communication channels you feel at ease with and genuinely enjoy. Hate giving prepared speeches? Participate in a panel or a podcast instead. Not that jazzed about writing an article? Document and publish a list of best practices.

And when you find activities you enjoy, amp up your ambitions. So, you delivered a well-received talk at work? Propose it to a professional conference. Wrote a long social media status update? Expand it into a blog post and add it to your LinkedIn profile. Or go bolder still, and submit an article to a company or industry newsletter. Climb further out on that limb, and be more widely seen.

Whatever your authentic style, there are ways to promote your accomplishments. You have permission to disregard 90 percent of the suggestions in this chapter and choose the activities that best fit your style. Then weave them in to the fabric of your everyday work so they become a nonevent.

Rule 3. Cater to the Culture

To further refine your approach to amplifying accomplishments, look at how your organization's culture calls attention to successes.

I've delivered workshops to employees of a midwestern manufacturer of heavy agricultural equipment and to employees at an international investment bank in New York. I can't tell you precisely which methods of promoting accomplishments go over best in either organization, but I know they're different.

Take the time to observe who gets rewarded at all levels of your organization, and reverse engineer how these employees make their value visible. Evaluate whether that approach could fit your style. Once you've identified what works, extrapolate what else might play well.

Examine what lies at the intersection of your organization's culture and the authentic ways you've identified to promote your accomplishments, and apply what you learn. For example, I spoke at a financial tech firm where one participant suggested, "Set up a Slack channel for recognizing team achievements." Her colleagues nodded in agreement. Same company, different location, and the group pounced on the idea of sending status reports to a distribution list of people who would benefit from being kept in the loop.

OWN IT

Three Rules of Thumb for Amplifying Accomplishments

- Choose two high-value accomplishments that reflect your brand.
- Choose a way to promote each accomplishment that authentically fits your style.
- Confirm that your strategy works in your organization's culture. Then go for it!

If you're stuck for ideas, hang tight. I'll share a bunch of suggestions later in this chapter. But first, fasten your seatbelt. This ride's about to get bumpy.

THE SOUL-CRUSHING TRUTH ABOUT WOMEN AND SELF-PROMOTION

As I mentioned at the beginning of this chapter, making achievements visible is a vital advancement strategy, especially for women, who often need to go to greater lengths to prove their competence. There's a further complication, though, and it's more fraught because it's gender specific.

It's been well documented that women tend to be reluctant to share their own accomplishments, while at the same time they're eager to celebrate and promote someone else's.[3] This reluctance is *not* a personal failing as much as it is a rational response to cultural norms. Self-promote and we might risk incurring disapproval for defying the social norm of "the nice girl."

While assertive self-advocacy lines up nicely with the long-standing stereotype of the ambitious male go-getter, some studies show that when women demonstrate identical behaviors, they elicit negative reactions for failing to show stereotypical "feminine traits" (such as being humble, nurturing, and collaborative). As a result of this disapproval, some women miss out on leadership opportunities.[4]

In some organizations, women face an exasperating double bind: self-advocate, and be sidelined for lacking social skills. Fail to self-advocate, and have your competence questioned.

Not surprisingly, women who fear this backlash are less vocal in claiming credit for their work.[5] If you've become wary of spotlighting your successes, this gender-bias penalty might be the culprit. Evaluate whether this backlash is your reality. If you suspect the problem is not you, it's the culture, the next section contains workaround strategies or ways to raise your visibility without the backlash.

And if you're someone who's accrued some significant influence and respect in your organization, you're in a strong position to become a game changer, by using your clout to publicly recognize other women and what they've done. If you're willing to stick your neck out, you *can* make a difference, bust biases, and shift your organization's culture.[6] When influential women lead by example and encourage others to assertively call attention to their performance, it becomes expected, rewarded, and normalized.

TEN STRATEGIES FOR STEALTH-PROMOTION

In a perfect world, we'd all be unapologetically vocal about what we do well, but that's not always possible. If your gut or your real-world experience tells you that's not going to fly, or if it feels awkward or inauthentic, that's OK. I trust your judgment, and you should too.

There are plenty of ways to make your value visible without triggering the backlash some women face when they overtly self-promote. How? Don't kowtow to cultural expectations. *Weaponize them* by taking full advantage of the stereotype of women as selfless and communal workers. Call it "stealth-promotion," not "self-promotion." You can be a brand builder *and* a bias buster. Here are 10 ways to ensure that your voice is heard, your brand is visible, and your accomplishments get acknowledged.

Don't even *think* of attempting to use them all. Choose the ones that are authentic to your style and fit well within your organization's culture. Some will even combat bias in the long term by making the idea of women promoting their value so common it's unremarkable, and they'll set a new baseline of expected behavior.

Stealth-Promotion Tactic 1.
Create a Consistent Identity

For some quick and easy wins within the walls of your workplace, prominently feature your leadership brand statement in one or more of these:

- Your employee profile on your organization's intranet
- The tagline on your email signature
- Your business cards
- The opening slide of any presentation
- Your professional bio

Next, mirror that presence with an equally consistent message in your social media profiles. For example, if your headline on LinkedIn is just your job title, you're missing an easy branding opportunity.

It's tough to accurately self-assess how you're coming across on all of these platforms, so ask a friend to conduct a "brand audit." Without revealing what your brand statement is, ask your friend to review the above items. Ask, "Based on what you see, what do you think my personal brand is?" Get that person's opinion on whether you're sending a consistent message.

Stealth-Promotion Tactic 2.
Upgrade Your Elevator Speech

Your elevator speech is your verbal business card—a way to reinforce your brand every time you introduce (or reintroduce) yourself to others. To create a memorable elevator speech, include these three main elements:

1. Your name, job title, and leadership brand statement.
2. A crisp overview of three responsibilities that support your brand statement. For example, say, "I am responsible for *a*, *b*, and *c*," where *a*, *b*, and *c* are straightforward, concise bullets points.
3. Finish with a statement like, "Come directly to me whenever you need *x*, *y*, and *z*."

Make yours the verbal equivalent of "dressing for the job you want" by describing not only what you do now but also what you're capable of doing next. Here are two ways to punch up your elevator speech to reflect your potential:

Be the go-to person for the bigger picture. Ditch the low-level tasks. Refer instead to your leadership skills, the higher-level value you add, and ways you go beyond your current job description.

Use strong, active leadership verbs. To shift perception of yourself from doer to leader, catch yourself before you say you "work on" something or even that you're "responsible for" it. Say you "lead," "direct," "oversee," "run," "orchestrate," "supervise," "head up," or are "in charge."

Your goal is to hear your brand boomerang back at you, when people describe to you in the terms you threw out.

Stealth-Promotion Tactic 3.
Give Progress Updates

Anytime you attack a new project, role, or assignment that aligns with your leadership brand, the results you deliver can reinforce your credibility— if you begin with that end in mind.

Before you begin work, speak with your management to clarify what's expected and what "great" looks like to them. But don't stop at that. Think expansively about whom you could gather input from and engage a wider set of stakeholders, customers, and other key people you'd like to build stronger ties to.

Ask "Mind if I keep you updated?" and "How frequently shall I check in?" so it's not only acceptable to check in later to share your progress, but expected. It's not self-promoting, it's *updating*.

"Don't go under the radar," says Kokko CEO Nina Bhatti. "Stay in contact, and make sure people are aware of what you're delivering to the organization."

Stealth-Promotion Tactic 4.
Become a Hub for Knowledge

Remember the Visible Experts, the industry rock stars from Chapter 3 who command fees many times that of their peers? When customers were asked to name the benefits of working with such stars, their top answer might surprise you. Sure, they solved more problems, got things done more rapidly, and generate previously unthought of solutions. But the most-cited benefit was: "We learn just from working with them."[7]

Says brand strategist Liz Harr, "People might not initially seek you out because they want to be educated. But in retrospect, they will identify learning from you as a top benefit of working with you."

When sales exec Alice Katwan was an individual contributor with an open-source software company, she organized lunchtime sessions to share what she was learning from her interactions with customers. The sessions were intended for newbies, but they became so popular they attracted senior accounts reps who wanted to learn from Alice's experiences too. Alice rapidly, albeit inadvertently, picked up a following.

When we brainstorm ways to promote accomplishments in my workshops, sharing knowledge is by far the most popular. The value to others is indisputable. If you're a thought leader, becoming a knowledge hub is an especially on-brand way for you to make your value visible.

Stealth-Promotion Tactic 5.
Speak the F Word

So you bombed the big presentation, missed a product rollout deadline, or had your new team implode. What now?

Don't be afraid of the F word: *failure*. Don't hide your face-plants, flops, and fails. Just like a dreadful first date can become a hilarious story with the addition of 24 hours, a girlfriend, and a bottle of Pinot, your most gut-wrenching failures can become part of your brand.

Mallun Yen is founder of Operator Collective, a venture capital fund. When Mallun was one of the youngest vice presidents at Cisco, she was a last-minute invitee to a meeting with a foreign government delegation. When one of the visitors turned to Mallun with a question on a highly sensitive topic, she wasn't sure what to say. "I panicked and babbled. I kept talking and talking," says Mallun. The experience was awful, and she wanted to run and hide. Fortunately for her, Mallun's boss encouraged her to work on her public speaking skills, and that kicked off her journey to becoming a confident, polished speaker. It's a story she's often shared.

The best learning opportunities sometimes come brilliantly disguised as a gut-wrenching, cringe-inducing flops. Your failures make for indelible, relatable lessons. To make a "flopportunity" part of your brand, tell an inspiring story about what went wrong and how you turned things around. This approach is especially effective for results leaders.

Like any good movie, a good story starts by setting the scene. Then there's some tension, which is resolved by the final act. Craft a memorable anecdote using the SPAR model, a common technique for answering job interview questions, which describes the following:

S: Situation

P: Problem

A: Action

R: Result

Don't cut too quickly to the end result: you'll shortchange the most interesting part. Here's one place in business where it pays to bring the drama. After setting the scene, describe the failure. Dramatize it. Pause for effect. This emotional roller-coaster ride is what makes your story unforgettable.

The technique works well for your accomplishments, too, but trust me: your mess-ups will be much more memorable.

Stealth-Promotion Tactic 6.
Promote a Problem

Don't just tell people what you do. Help them *feel* it. A well-told story will be remembered more accurately for far longer than a laundry list of facts.[8] That's why storytelling is one of the best ways to highlight great work.

If one of your signature accomplishments is a problem you solved, you should be telling the story (especially if you're a change leader). People care a lot more about their problems than your brand, so promote the problem your brand can or has solved. Focus on problems you were born to solve. To other people, these are headaches or catastrophes, but they get you fired up and inspired to say, "Step aside" so you can have at it.

The SPAR model (situation, problem, action, result) works equally well when crafting a memorable story about a problem as it does when talking about a failure. When people experience a similar problem, they'll be more likely to remember you, the expert who can solve it.

Stealth-Promotion Tactic 7.
Galvanize a Community

Serpil Bayraktar is a distinguished engineer at Cisco Systems and founder of Cisco's Women in Technology Program, a community of women who care deeply about technology and get together to discuss important technical topics and hear from other experts.

She's on a personal mission to increase the number of women at all levels of technical leadership. Being a role model to others in the program was a partial motivator for her own path into senior leadership and becoming one of a small handful of women at her company to achieve the highest technical rank, that of distinguished engineer.

With a supportive community you can test opinions, develop a point of view, amplify your voice, and become a highly visible leader. You can also build the association between your name and a larger cause.

To galvanize your own community, get to know others who share your interests, solve similar problems, or care about a common cause. Identify a cause or mission aligned with your brand that you're passionate about and that is meaningful to others too. You can join a group, start a group, volunteer on the leadership team of a professional association, or bring experts in to speak to your team.

> There's a lot you can accomplish by yourself, but if you want to do bigger things, it's going to take a community.

If you're a thought leader, this is another top strategy for promoting your expertise. As Serpil says, "I really admire thought leaders who focus on something bigger than themselves." There's a lot you can accomplish by yourself, but if you want to do bigger things, it's going to take a community.

Stealth-Promotion Tactic 8.
Seek out Awards

External recognition confers clout. It's one thing to be a researcher, but another thing entirely to be an *award-winning researcher*. Add one or two more awards and you have a *multi-award-winning researcher*.

You've read some good examples in this book. Diversity and inclusion leader Sara Sperling was recognized on *Business Insider*'s list of "31 Most Important LGBT People in Tech," and customer strategy exec Allison Unkraut was honored with a "Top Women in Grocery" award.

In public relations, this is known as "third-party validation," which is another way of saying that when someone else toots your horn, it's seen as more credible than when you toot it yourself.

Be Leaderly polled 200 professionals and found their biggest hesitation to go after awards or other external recognition was not their perceived lack of expertise. Fully 65 percent said it was the awkwardness of nominating themselves. Our poll also suggested that respondents would be more comfortable applying if their company celebrated such achievements or they received encouragement from their manager.

If you're starting out, look for ways to earn internal recognition, spot awards, and company honors. As your body of work expands, go after industry-level recognition. Awkward as it feels, summon the moxie to self-nominate more. Or write up the paperwork for a friend to submit, and return the favor. Encourage others to go after awards too, and celebrate when they win.

Stealth-Promotion Tactic 9.
Ignite Posse Power

Don't underestimate the power of banding together with other women to smash social norms around recognition. At a conference for human resources professionals, I heard a panel of women recount how a decade earlier, when they were frequently the only women in meetings at a consumer products company, they formed a support squad. They backed each other's ideas in meetings, called attention to each other's accomplishments, and nominated each other for highly visible roles. It worked. Looking back, they credit the power of their posse as a contributing factor in their subsequent advancement. They each now hold senior HR leadership roles.

You might have heard this stealthy style of clapping back at bias referred to as "amplification," a strategy used by women in the Obama administration to ensure that their voices were heard. When one woman raised an idea that was not picked up on, another would repeat it while giving credit to the colleague who originated it. As amplification became common practice, the president took note, which led to an even more visible result: more women in top aide and departmental leadership roles.[9]

Stealth-Promotion Tactic 10.
Be a Hero Maker

When Stephanie Matthews first left broadcast news for a new career in public relations, she felt uncomfortable promoting her accomplishments, even though she recognized the necessity. Then she came up with a work-around: brag about what her team was doing, knowing it would build up team members' confidence and reflect well on her too. "Talking about great things we were doing together, a little bit at a time, helped build a case for the value of our work," says Stephanie.

Soon she was calling out what her direct reports were working on, bringing attention to their collective accomplishments, and publicly acknowledging the group for delivering great work. Says Stephanie, "We call it 'forwardable praise.' I'll ask leaders to write up a glowing email about the team's accomplishments that we can all forward up the chain to their bosses' bosses."

When you make heroes out of others and use a "cooperative brag" for accomplishments that are tied with your own, you'll not only raise your profile, but also boost the motivation and engagement of everyone around you. And more praise leads to higher team performance.[10]

When you stand up and acknowledge others, everyone wins. If you're a people leader or change leader, focus on team members and other collaborators. If you're a service leader, use similar techniques with your customers or constituency.

33 WAYS TO AMPLIFY YOUR ACCOMPLISHMENTS

Remember: It's not enough to be it if no one can see it.

There's no lack of techniques you can use to amplify the accomplishments that align with your aspirations. Here's a big-ass list of 33 specific ways you can get started now:

1. Forward a message where someone thanks you for something you've done well to your boss and your boss's boss. Add the three simple letters FYI before hitting send.
2. Take what worked and made a big impact in one area and reproduce those best practices in another area.
3. Frame and display a diploma, certificate, or photograph that represents an achievement.
4. Feature your leadership brand in your employee profile, email signature, business cards, presentations, bio, and social media profiles.
5. Upgrade your elevator speech to reflect your brand *and* potential.
6. Update a key leader or stakeholder on your progress toward a goal.
7. Start sending regular status reports to a distribution list of people who would appreciate being kept up to date.
8. Create a presentation on best practices to share with other teams.
9. Contribute an article to your organization's newsletter or an industry publication.
10. Invite a leader to a team meeting to hear what you and your colleagues are working on.
11. Ask a well-thought-out question at a meeting that shows what you know.
12. Ask for a spot on a meeting agenda to share updates, knowledge, or lessons learned.
13. Write a social media humblebrag.
14. Write a blog post. If you don't have a blog, post it on your LinkedIn profile.
15. Give a webinar or lunchtime talk, and include examples of your work.

16. Make an instructional video.
17. Be a podcast guest.
18. Give a conference presentation or join a panel.
19. Remind people you're always happy to answer questions about your area of expertise.
20. Use the SPAR method to tell a story about a flopportunity or an important problem you solved.
21. Start a group whose mission is linked to your brand.
22. Volunteer on the leadership team of a professional association.
23. Self-nominate for awards and recognition.
24. Ask a colleague, manager, or mentor to nominate you for an award. (Offer to do the paperwork.)
25. Team up with a group of colleagues and nominate each other for awards and recognition.
26. Back your posse's ideas in meetings, and call attention to each other's accomplishments.
27. Create "forwardable praise," a glowing email about team accomplishments to forward up the management chain.
28. Start meetings by asking each individual to share a recent accomplishment or best practice.
29. Set up a Slack channel for recognizing team members' achievements.
30. Use the SPAR model to tell the story of a problem the team conquered.
31. Frame and hang documents or photographs that represent a group achievement.
32. Write five recommendations for others on LinkedIn. (I can pretty much guarantee someone will write one for you in return.)
33. Put together a presentation on a team win or best practices. Bring others along to copresent it to management, in a learning session, or to other groups.

Download a printable version of this list at jomiller.com/amplify.

OWN IT

33 Ways to Amplify Your Accomplishments

- Start keeping a running list of accomplishments rather than trying to remember them at performance review time.
- Pick a few of the 33 suggestions that fit well with your brand and your organization's culture.
- Identify any additional ways you could amplify your accomplishments.
- Try out one of these ideas this week.

OUTSOURCE IT

Build a Hero-Making Machine

When a team's culture celebrates achievement, everyone gets to worry less about promoting their own achievements. Ask your manager if team meetings can include more activities that recognize accomplishments and excellence. If you manage a team, task team members with organizing regular recognition activities.

BUILD A CASE FOR YOUR VALUE

Very few people, including your manager and colleagues, will have the luxury of time to observe your work closely. Most of the time, all they have to go on is what they hear. So it's vital that you're practiced at articulating your value and contributions.

There's another lesson here too: when you make your value visible, you empower your future negotiations and career moves.

Diane Gonzalez had been with a previous company for some time when she realized her salary hadn't kept pace

> **When you make your value visible, you empower your future negotiations and career moves.**

with the market. "I believed that based on my contributions, track record, and domain expertise, I deserved a raise," says Diane, who is now vice president of the Amazon Web Services (AWS) commerce platform.

Diane did her homework, taking four steps to build a solid case for her value:

- Documenting the value that she was bringing into the organization
- Researching what other companies were paying for someone with her skills
- Crafting her case, sticking to the facts about her value to the organization
- Preparing to answer anticipated follow-up questions

She set up a meeting with her manager and presented her case. The result: She negotiated a substantial raise.

If you believe you aren't being compensated for your value, you really to owe it to yourself to ask for a raise, says Diane. "Remember, there are pretty significant costs associated with hiring someone new to a team, so it's expensive to replace someone. The knowledge that walks out the door can take years for the company to rebuild."

CHAPTER 7 WRAP-UP

No matter how urgent, important, or never-ending your workload is, you can't afford to spend 100 percent of your working hours with your head down, working hard, even if you're accomplishing great things. *Especially* if you're accomplishing great things. Commit to spending an hour a week, less than 3 percent of your working time, making yourself, your brand, and your accomplishments visible.

One workshop participant described this comprehensive approach as the opposite of speed dating, saying, "My aha moment was that making yourself known in the organization is like a slow dating process. It requires courting, because not everyone sees you the way you see yourself."

You'll know you've succeeded when people, unprompted, refer to you in a way that reflects your leadership brand. So, make it your ultimate goal to inspire comments like these:

- Priya *turns breakthrough ideas into profitable contracts.*
- Natalia, you're our *cultural change agent.* How would you approach the issue?
- The online commerce team needs a *negotiation strategist.* Would Louise be interested?

When others tell your story for you, that's when you know that it's working.

Your work doesn't speak for itself. When you keep your head down, you silence your voice and submerge your influence. Raise your voice. Communicate your brand. Make your value visible. Amplify your accomplishments. Heck, even promote your failures. And keep at it until your old brand is cancelled.

In the final two chapters, learn how to build a coalition of people to support you.

Mobilizing Your Support Squad

You don't have to make this climb alone. In this section, you'll address the question, "Whose help can I enlist?"

You'll develop some new political savvy and cultivate a well-rounded, influential network of collaborators, allies, and sponsors.

The two chapters within Part III will help you gather the allies you need to thrive. Here's what to expect:

- *Chapter 8, Rally Your Crew: The Four People You Need in Your Corner.* This chapter explores why trust is the foundation for influence, and why relationship building must come before leading. You'll create a strategic networking plan and explore four categories of people who make up a well-rounded, influential network.

- *Chapter 9, Attract Influential Advocates: Enlist Support to Kick Down Doors.* If there's a closed door between you and your next career breakthrough, an influential advocate can open it. Learn what sponsorship is, why it's frequently overlooked, and how it is earned.

Rally Your Crew

The Four People You Need in Your Corner

> *You have to connect with people and build trust*
> *before you can influence or lead them.*
> *Trust is the conduit for influence; it's the medium*
> *through which ideas travel.*[1]
> **—Amy Cuddy,**
> social psychologist

Let's take a look at the most important asset you will build in your career. No, I'm not talking about the funds in your retirement account. I'm talking about an exclusive subset of your professional network—your inner circle, what I call your "support squad."

Who are they? They are your close collaborators and the people who inspire, challenge, and motivate you to make bold, fearless moves. They're the people you partner with to make a larger impact than you can make alone.

Building relationships is not something that chitchatting slackers do to avoid getting real work done. Developing these bonds, in a mindful and meaningful way, is not only part of your job. It is *the real work* of leadership. Because how else would you make an outsized impact that far exceeds what you could deliver on your own?

"Surround yourself with people who support you, advise you, help you, and build you up," says open source thought leader Nithya Ruff. Even if you're a star performer, your progress will stall if you try to go it alone. Every leader has their moment of realization about just how much more can be achieved through collaboration, and every leader needs a core group of strong connections to stay grounded.

MISSTEP 9

The moments you spend strengthening these ties are an investment that will pay off by making every other hour of your week more productive. Career Misstep 9 is *working when you should be relationship building*. Neglect your network, and you'll only make more work for yourself.

The Leaderly Move is *building a supportive, influential network*. In this chapter, we'll cover practical steps and insights for rallying your core crew of collaborators and allies.

A PRECIOUS, PRECIOUS RESOURCE

When I surveyed my workshop participants, 92 percent said they are on good terms with those whose input they rely on to get their work done. But only 40 percent said they have an *influential* network of mentors and advocates supporting their career growth.

There's a wealth of research to support the value of investing in relationships. Here are some findings that stand out:

- The McKinsey Leadership Project studied what drives and sustains the most successful female leaders. One of the strongest traits they shared was *connecting*, defined as "identifying who can help you grow, building stronger relationships, and increasing your sense of belonging."[2]
- The project's authors also pointed out that people with strong networks and good mentors enjoy more promotions, higher pay, and greater career satisfaction. (Who wouldn't want more of all three?)

- Dr. Christina Maslach, who devoted her career to studying work-related burnout, found that the best prevention comes from the human connections we make. She calls our social network, where each of you have each other's back, "a precious, precious resource."[3]
- And in case you needed one more reason for forming a close-knit girl gang, there's now research to confirm that having an inner circle of female contacts helps women overcome bias and other cultural hurdles to reach higher levels of leadership and compensation.[4]

Whichever way you look at it, these relationships are utterly essential to your success—especially when you're leading without positional authority.

DON'T BE A LONE INFLUENCER

Early in her career, human resources leader Liz Brenner was put in charge of a big portion of a high-priority, cross-functional project. The catch: No one would directly report to her. It was a classic case of having to influence without authority. So one of Liz's first moves was to build trust with the people on her unofficial project team. Liz set up formal meetings to explain the situation, describe her ideas, and gather feedback. She also made it a point to have coffee with people for more informal conversations. The approach paid off. As people got to know Liz, they came around to supporting her and her project. Slowly, they got on board with her plans.

If you want to expand your scope of influence, Liz recommends building a strong network and taking every opportunity to practice selling your ideas and building trust.

Having a bright idea—even if you're right—isn't enough to get people to follow you. I remember having a conversation with the chief technology officer of a public company about influencing, and she described how she had seen too many projects led by great, passionate people fail because they tried to be a lone influencer.

To grasp just how essential relationships are to influencing without positional authority, imagine trying to get anything significant done without them.

Let's say you need someone's help to move forward with a project that's at a standstill, but you don't know that person very well. I hope you're up for a challenge because here's what it might take:

- First, you need to convince that person the conversation is worth her time and wrangle a spot on her calendar.
- Then you need to prepare for the conversation and come up with a strategy for pitching your request.
- You'll need to contemplate what objections the person might raise, how to overcome any concerns, how to persuade her to help you, and what would motivate her to take action. But *you don't know her yet*, so you'll just have to guess.

You know what's a *lot* of hard work? Convincing someone to do something when you don't have a preexisting relationship. Depending on the person, it can feel like cajoling, pushing, and begging. And pleading ain't leading.

Now imagine the person whose help you'd like to enlist knows you well. Perhaps she's already worked with you and she has seen the quality of your work firsthand. She can vouch for your character, and she'll know you're committed to doing the right thing by the organization. Or maybe you've gone out of your way to get to know her, the problems she's trying to solve, and what drives and motivates her. Or you've assisted her with something that was meaningful to her. She knows you've got her back. In any of these cases, you might not need to sweat over preparing a persuasive pitch—it could be as *simple as asking*.

You don't have to be a born networker to have a killer network, but I'm not going to sugarcoat it: it requires effort. You'll need to invest the time, social energy, and emotional commitment to develop strong, trusting, mutually supportive *personal relationships*. For some people, this comes easily. For others, it's the most challenging part of being a leader—especially if you're an introvert and interacting with people depletes you. But I can assure you that as your network of deep

> **You don't have to be a born networker to have a killer network, but I'm not going to sugarcoat it: it requires effort.**

relationships expands, so will your ability to collaborate, influence, and make great stuff happen—in other words, lead.

Bottom line: Trying to lead as a lone influencer is the hardest way to get things done.

THE CONDUIT FOR INFLUENCE

"We started out as cube neighbors at the beginning of my corporate career," says Joanne Collins of her former colleague at a life reinsurance firm. The colleague, Gabe, would often overhear Joanne talking to clients on the phone and helping new employees. Since he was more of an introvert, Gabe valued Joanne's ease with relationship building. To Joanne, who is now senior vice president of client services for RegEd, Gabe became a trusted source of feedback and valuable career guidance. And he often sought out her input on work policies or staffing issues.

The working relationship continued for many years, even as Gabe rose through the ranks in a series of increasingly senior roles. "This foundation of trust was built on his seeing me in action when I didn't know I was being watched," says Joanne. Later, Gabe became the best manager she has ever had, then a mentor, and her first sponsor. It shows you never know when the opportunity to build trust will appear and where it's going to take you in your career.

As a leader, trust is everything.

Having the greatest idea is worth nothing without trust, says social psychologist, author, and Harvard lecturer Dr. Amy Cuddy. "Trust is the conduit for influence; it's the medium through which ideas travel. If (people) don't trust you, your ideas are just dead in the water." says Amy.[5] You've got to gain trust before you can influence. Connect before you collaborate. Listen before you lead. Partner before you persuade.

But don't confuse building trust with making friends.

Says Joanne, "You won't be friends with everyone you work with." It's more important to have relationships that are built on honesty, integrity, and openness. "All relationships need trust. Everyone wants to feel heard and feel important," says Joanne, a masterful

> **Connect before you collaborate. Listen before you lead. Partner before you persuade.**

connector and relationship nurturer whose previous job title was vice president of relationships management. Only once trust is established can you move on to making requests, identifying areas of mutual interest, and creating shared goals.

"If you want to build trust with someone, come to the table with open intent," says Joanne. Here are her top six suggestions for how to develop trusting relationships at work:

- **Be candid and authentic.** Always be open and honest about your motives.
- **Put yourself in their shoes.** Try to understand what motivates others—and what turns them off.
- **Give more than you get.** This can't be a one-way street. A trusting relationship is built on value to both parties.
- **Open yourself up to input.** Ask for feedback and be prepared to listen and respond, especially if it challenges your thinking.
- **Avoid gossiping or venting to third parties.** Communicate any issues directly with the individual involved.
- **Don't make assumptions.** If you don't understand a person's motivation or why he is doing what he's doing, ask for clarification.

For a simple thought experiment to gauge whether you've built trust with any particular person, ask yourself, "If either of us needed anything, would it be as simple as asking?" If the answer's yes, you've got trust.

OWN IT

Building Trust

Assess whether you've built trust with a person at work who's important to you by asking yourself, "If either of us needed anything, would it be as simple as asking?"

If the answer's no or not quite, review the six suggestions for developing trusting relationships, and choose one or more to work on now.

POLITICAL SMARTS

Here's a reality check, though. You won't be friends with everyone you work with, and you won't gain everyone's trust either.

I hope you ate your Wheaties because this is not a topic to tackle on an empty stomach. I'm talking about office politics.

The *Merriam-Webster* online dictionary defines *office politics* as "the activities, attitudes, or behaviors that are used to get or keep power or an advantage within a business or company."[6] If that's too clinical for your liking, think of it as the interactions, undercurrents, cliques, hierarchies, hidden alliances, and fiefdoms that can be empowering and helpful when they go your way—and confusing, annoying, or toxic as hell when they don't.

Office politics: You can't live with them, but you also can't do business without them.

My guess is you don't exactly jump out of bed every morning, thrilled to go to work and play political games. If you find dealing with office politics difficult and painful, would it help to know you're not alone? Because you're not—far from it:

- When LinkedIn surveyed 950 professional women, nearly 3 out of 4 cited office politics as their biggest frustration.[7]
- In my survey of 1,200 workshop participants, only 1 in 25 (!) strongly agreed that they knew how to navigate office politics in a positive, effective way.
- Research reveals that many female managers feel engaging in political behavior is difficult and painful. Some even viewed it as "evil."[8]

I could go on. But instead, let me say that if you've had to gut out a situation at work that felt evil, you have my sympathy. No one should have to put up with that, yet many of the women I've spoken to find it hard to imagine how dealing with office politics can be anything other than unpleasant. So it will come as no surprise that when I asked workshop participants to describe their biggest career obstacles they said this:

- I want to effectively navigate through the political maze without compromising my integrity.

- In order to stay away from politics, I often let go of opportunities.
- My challenge is successfully surviving and being effective at coleading a very large, politically charged enterprisewide project.
- I struggle to navigate office politics and achieve my personal goals without burning bridges.

Again, I could go on.

So why not just ignore office politics?

Well, here's the uncomfortable truth of it: as author Erin Burt notes, "Avoiding politics altogether can be *deadly for your career*. Every workplace has an intricate system of power, and you can—and should—work it ethically to your best advantage."[9] I love that truthbomb of a quote. You *can* work this ethically, and not only to your advantage but also to the benefit of those around you too.

It's time to stop saying, "I don't do office politics." Here's why: politically skilled people *do better in their careers*. Research shows that people who are politically savvy enjoy better career prospects, experience better career trajectories, and are seen as more promotable.[10] They are also less likely to make the types of career-derailing errors that can clamp a lid on future prospects.

> It's time to stop saying, "I don't do office politics."

"A person rarely gets promoted without having developed strong political skills," says Florida State University management professor Pamela Perrewé.[11] But people who have these skills aren't stereotypical master manipulators. Here's the jaw-dropping truth: political skill can be a force for good. "Positive political savvy" is a leadership skill, and it can be learned.

MISSTEP 10

Avoiding office politics is Misstep 10.

You don't have to recoil from office politics, and you don't need to become a political beast that you cringe to look at in the mirror. A Leaderly Move you can make instead is *practicing positive political skills*.

I'm sure you can think of a role model who does this masterfully: a leader or colleague who is unafraid to dive into the political fray, yet somehow resurfaces with her or his integrity and relationships intact. Think about who that individual is and identify some qualities or characteristics that allow that person to thrive.

Drawing on two decades of research into organizational politics, Pamela, coauthor of *Political Skill at Work*, identified four skills used by people who are positively political:

- Networking ability
- Sincerity
- Interpersonal influence
- Social astuteness

In other words, if you want positive political smarts, focus on fostering relationships of trust, connecting in a way that others find sincere, and developing a persuasive leadership style. And while you're at it, become a keen observer of social dynamics, a bit like a corporate anthropologist. You won't dissolve politics, but you can certainly disarm plenty of it.

If it helps, cancel the phrase "office politics" from your vocabulary. It's loaded with negativity and leads many of us to recoil from politically charged situations. Instead, think about building the leadership skill of *organizational astuteness*. In the next section, I'll share a tool for honing that skill.

OWN IT

Positive Political Savvy

- Review the four career benefits of being politically skilled (better career prospects, better career trajectory, being more promotable, and being less likely to derail). Pick one that's more important to you, and let it feed your determination to confront office politics with grace and grit.
- Identify a role model who navigates office politics in a positive, effective way, and think of three qualities or characteristics that allow that person to navigate successfully. Identify one action you'll take to emulate her or his approach.

- Do a quick self-assessment on the four components of positive political savvy: networking ability, sincerity, influence, and social astuteness. Identify one you want to improve on, and commit to finding opportunities over the next week to practice.

THE SHADOW ORGANIZATION MAP

Your org chart has its uses, like showing who's on your team and who reports to whom. But there's a lot of useful information that's missing. For example, you probably know colleagues whose influence outweighs their job title and who are the first people you'd go to for help if you needed to influence the thinking of the greater team. But staring at your org chart won't reveal that.

Here's a more effective tool for developing your organizational astuteness—a key component of positive political skill. I call this the "shadow organization map," and I've repeatedly heard it's one of the most useful and practical takeaways from my workshops.

To create your shadow organization map, you'll need to think like an amateur social scientist, observing and documenting the behavior, relationships, and communication of those around you. To see examples and a video, visit www.jomiller.com/shadowmap. To create yours, I recommend going old school with paper and a range of writing and drawing tools—pens, pencils, markers, crayons—in a variety of colors. If you can't tackle this hands-on exercise right now, plan to come back to it later. I guarantee it will be worth your while.

Org chart: Draw a quick sketch of your org chart. Include yourself, your manager, your boss's boss, and up to 10 people you work with the most. If they're not in your immediate team, add them off to one side. Make the chart large—fill the page.

Add the following five elements to the org chart you just drew to transform it into a shadow organization map.

Relationships: Using one of your color pens, pencils, or crayons, draw a solid line connecting any two people who have a good, strong working relationship. Continue until you've noted all the positive relationships this way. Then use a dashed line to denote any relationships that are broken. Include yourself in this step and the subsequent ones.

It can be useful to ask yourself, "How did these relationships form, and what's the glue that maintains them?" Or "How did this relationship get damaged, and what perpetuates the dysfunction?" Notice if this suggests ways to work more effectively with those people.

Influence: Take out a new color, and add arrows showing which direction influence moves between each pair of people on your chart. Influence doesn't only trickle downward, so look out for instances where people are "influencing upward" effectively. Where two people are equally influential, show arrows going in both directions.

Coalitions: Take another a new color, and draw a misshapen circle around any groups of three or more people who have formed a supportive group and are freely sharing information, resources, and opportunities.

It can be useful to ask yourself, "How did these coalitions form, and what's the glue that maintains them?" Set aside any preconceptions like "They're all finance nerds" or "It's a boys' club," because stereotypes like these can disempower you when it comes to working effectively with those groups or individuals. See if there's a better explanation. For example, they may have worked together on an intense project, or perhaps they share a common interest or work style. Keep looking for any hints for working more effectively with them.

Influencers: Grab a different color. Every team or organization has influencers who are skilled at changing minds, driving change, and making things happen. It's incredibly useful to know who they are. Identify any key influencers on your map by giving them a little halo, or, if they're a negative influencer, a set of horns. (By the way, this map is for your eyes only.)

Sponsorships: Pick your last color, and identify any people who have direct managers who are developing them and throwing career opportunities their way. This is sponsorship, and Chapter 9 explores how it works. For now, draw a little ladder connecting a person to her or his sponsor. Note if there are any sponsorship relationships spanning multiple levels too. If you've ever been sponsored, you'll know what a dynamic and exhilarating experience it can be. Note whether *you* have any sponsors, or if there's potential for you to attract one.

Put your finishing touches on your shadow organization map by diagramming any final relationship lines, influence arrows, coalition circles, halos or horns for key influencers, or sponsorship ladders. Reflect on anything you've learned, including any "epiphanettes." There's usually an aha! moment or two revealed by your map.

THE SHADOW ORGANIZATION MAP

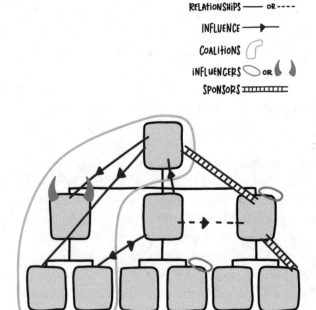

For example, one finance manager I coached had always detested office politics, but she found her lack of political awareness meant she was passed over for plum assignments. Her shadow map revealed her lack of strong relationship ties beyond her immediate work group. So she created a networking plan, started speaking up more, and made herself invaluable to an influential leader she'd previously been invisible to. In time, she became an influential voice in her own right, she earned a sponsor, and her career took off.

If you like the exercise, consider expanding it to include more people or teams. Definitely redraw your map anytime there's a change in the makeup of your work group. You'll regain your organizational astuteness more rapidly, and that will help you recover momentum in your role.

YOUR STRATEGIC NETWORKING PLAN

If you're looking for a way to become a stronger leader or influencer or to be more effective in your role, there's simply no substitute for developing stronger relationships with the people your work affects, even if you're in regular contact. Build relationships long before you think you'll need them, or you'll train people to hide when they see you approaching—not exactly optimal conditions.

Better yet, create a strategic networking plan. Take out another blank sheet of paper and draw a line down the middle. Label the left column "Who" and the right column "How." In the "Who" column list at least six people you should get to know or build a stronger relationship with. Next to each name, in the column labeled "How," add one specific action you'll take to develop the relationship and build their trust.[12]

Here's an example from Lee, a marketing director whose goal was to move to a different area of her company where she could be more entrepreneurial:

Who	How
Nadia, division head	Attend end-of-quarter BBQ. Request an informational meeting.
Raj, skip-level manager	Arrive early or stay late in staff meetings.
Michele, product design engineer	Invite for lunch.
Stefan, chief of operations	Ask HR for invitation to next executive roundtable.

Remember the definition of *strategy* from Chapter 5: having a long-term plan and putting it into action. To make your networking plan truly strategic, focus on an important career or leadership goal before working through the steps of the Own It exercise that follows. If you don't yet know a specific person's name, jot down a job title or team as a placeholder. Add at least one person who's a bit "scary," as Lee did for the chief of operations.

But remember the paradox of networking: you won't gain true allies by being calculating. Set aside your agenda, and develop each relationship with open intent. Trust can't be forced, only earned.

By patiently working her plan, Lee, the marketing director, gained a mentor in Nadia, the head of a different business division. Later, with Nadia's encouragement, Lee applied for a role in a new product group with growth potential. Within a year, Lee had gained the startup experience she craved.

This exercise comes with a guarantee: If you get clear on your goal, craft a long-term relationship-building plan, and follow through, there will come a time when you never have to look for a job again. The job will find you.

OWN IT

Your Strategic Networking Plan

- To make your networking plan a strategic one, reflect on the lofty career or leadership goal you identified in Chapter 2, and consider whether your current network supports your goal. If not, identify any gaps in your network.
- Review your shadow organization map looking for additional gaps to fill.
- List at least six people to initiate or strengthen a relationship with and a specific tactic to develop each relationship. Take at least one action.
- While you're at it, use your elevator speech from Chapter 7 so people get to know your leadership brand.

FOUR TYPES OF ALLIES YOU NEED
IN YOUR NETWORK

Everyone needs a few influential allies. But if you work in an organization with hundreds or even thousands of people you could join forces with, or if this is the first time you've taken a strategic approach to networking, you might be wondering where to start.

When it comes to your network, size matters, but not in the way you'd think. One study found that executive leaders surround themselves with a relatively small number of close confidantes, a "critical few," fewer than 30, who make the biggest difference to their careers.[13]

We've been conditioned to think that more is better: more LinkedIn connections, more Instagram followers. You're probably overestimating the size and composition of an influential network. Focused and diverse beats broad and homogeneous. You don't need an extensive array of professional contacts, just a carefully curated inner circle—like a personal board of directors—who inspire, motivate, and support you to play big, lead boldly, and make sh!t happen. These are the ones to consult frequently for a multifaceted mix of advice, feedback, and assistance. Just as companies take great care in selecting their corporate board members, so should you.

Nehal Mehta, director of strategic partnerships with Genesys, takes an analytical approach to composing her board of directors. Whenever she takes on a new role or product, she will start with a "state of the union" assessment. Nehal asks herself, "What will I need to learn? What are the areas that I'm going to need to grow in? Who are my go-to people?" to see whether she is positioned for success. From there, she decides whom to reach out to.

Here's a caution though: try not to fall into the "like attracts like" trap. Expand your circle to include unlikely candidates. For example, some of your best partners could be your "coopetition"—colleagues you might otherwise tend to compete with or feel intimidated by, unless you identify a shared cause for cooperation. Also, own up to the "unstrengths" we talked about in Chapter 2, and actively look for people whose skills shore up your deficits. As Diane Janknegt, Amsterdam-based founder of kid-friendly search engine Wizenoze, says, "Look for people whose skills are the opposite of yours. Dare to emphasize your weaknesses."

To rally a truly supportive, influential crew, start with these four key types of allies. Make sure you've got at least one of each type in your network.

Ally 1. The Connector

Connectors make introductions and help you to grow your network.

A connector is a true "people person" who seems to know—and get along with—just about everyone. If you're taking tentative steps toward networking strategically for the first time, look for connectors first because they thrive on opening doors, making introductions, and helping others grow their networks.

Is there someone you know who can't resist matchmaking, always introducing people who could benefit from knowing each other? Consider her for the role of connector.

If you're looking for a connector, pay attention to who's at the hub of thriving social networks, professional communities, and even well-attended meetings.

Of course, trusting relationships are built on reciprocity and giving more value than you get, so find something you can do to help, and build credibility by offering something of value related to your area of expertise. Share knowledge, offer assistance, or introduce a connector to someone new. Then, share your interests and the types of people you're interested in meeting. Chances are your connector will be energized by the request. Connectors find it gratifying when people they introduce hit it off, so let them know what comes of the introductions they facilitate.

Add a connector or two to your strategic networking plan, and they'll help you grow your network. It's what they love to do.

Ally 2. The Informational Powerhouse

Informational powerhouses keep a finger on the pulse of what's going on in their organizations and in the broader business environment or industry. They can help you stay current on new trends, business developments, market shifts, resource reallocations, and so on. They are often first to know about seismic changes like reorgs and cutbacks. Discerning curators of relevant business information, they know what's gossip or noise and when to pay close attention. By checking in frequently with your informational powerhouses, you'll deepen your understanding of the broader business environment, and you'll find yourself making sound predictions and decisions more confidently and rapidly.

To find the informational powerhouses inside your company, pay attention to who connects the dots between day-to-day work and the larger strategy. Look for the deeply knowledgeable colleague whom everyone looks to for the final word in meetings because they are so well-versed, or the one acting as a bridge between cross-functional teams because her expertise spans across departments. At an industry level, informational powerhouses are the must-see futurist conference speakers or the people whose articles and tweets you keep up with because their analysis is so insightful.

Make sure you've got at least one informational powerhouse in your inner circle. You may find it useful to identify several, each with unique domains of expertise, or representing each of the five types of leaders: change, people, results, service, and thought.

Ally 3. The Influencer

Influencers help you make things happen in areas outside the scope of your own influence.

Influencers drive results. They get things done. They aren't necessarily high-level or high-profile leaders. Instead, they are the change makers found at all levels of an organization. If you need to reach beyond your personal scope of influence to get people on board with an idea or initiative, or persuade them to take action, line up support from your influencers.

When an influencer lends her or his voice to your cause, it reduces skepticism and fortifies your credibility. Influencers can provide the heavy-hitting support that can guarantee the success of your initiatives. They can help you understand your stakeholders' perspectives, how to engage them, and the best way to deliver your message.

Influencers are people who have earned the respect of their organizations. When they speak, people listen. To identify influencers, pay attention to who has this type of clout. Be on the lookout for those who are amplifying the voices of team members in meetings, advocating for their suggestions, and increasing the likelihood that those ideas are embraced and executed. And when teams get stuck, pay attention to the person they automatically look to for direction. Think about who you'd like to have your back when you encounter a roadblock, deliver a presentation, or submit a proposal. An influencer's show of support can bolster your credibility and clear the path forward.

Here are two strategies for working effectively with influencers.

1. Master the Meeting Before the Meeting

If you're preparing to deliver a big proposal or presentation, don't underestimate what can be accomplished in a meeting *before* the meeting. If there are key players whose opinions could sway a group's decision in your direction, securing their prior agreement might help you avoid walking in and getting blindsided, not walking away with the results you hoped for, or finding out they've already made up their minds.

Set up one-on-one meetings with influencers to preview your ideas and hear their concerns. Include them in your preparation so by the time the big meeting comes, they have a stake in your success. One corporate communications leader I spoke to suggested asking these questions:

- Is there anything I could explain more clearly?
- Is it something you agree with?
- Does this align with your initiatives? If not, why?
- And if it does, will you back me up when I deliver my presentation?

You might not enlist all key decision makers as your advocates. But, by preselling your ideas, you'll know who's neutral or skeptical and why, so you can address all points of view in your presentation. Plus, you'll have lined up a few influential advocates.

2. Don't Neglect Your Naysayers

Though it's human nature to avoid engaging with skeptics, naysayers, and/or people who challenge your thinking, don't fall into this trap. As one executive pointed out to me, they can be as pivotal to your success as the speck of sand that's the irritant an oyster needs to grow a pearl.

Betty Chan-Bauza was once recruited by a startup to bring strategic thinking to an established leadership team. Not long after joining, she had to give a large presentation to her peers. It was vital to make a good impression, but Betty could sense her counterpart in sales was not on board. She needed his support, or, at the very least, his lack of dissent. So she scheduled a face-to-face meeting with him on his own turf, in his office, to explain her thinking and solicit his thoughts and feedback with sincerity.

"In that meeting, I learned what a strategic mind he had," says Betty, now vice president of product management with Early Warning Services. Her colleague added valuable input, and they left the meeting having created a shared vision. He went on to become a long-term advocate and friend. Though they're now at different companies, they still do business together.

"My lesson learned was that strong relationships of mutual respect can be built through listening, learning, and striving toward a common goal," says Betty. Even the biggest skeptic can become a partner and advocate.

If you don't have an influencer or two in your network, think about who you'd like to add.

Ally 4. The Mentor

Mentors support your growth and development by providing advice, feedback, and guidance. They're the people you go to when you could use a confidence boost or sounding board for everyday situations, difficult problems, and almost any scenario in between.

"You need to have mentors in your network who give you different types of feedback," says Amanda Martinez, group vice president of corporate procurement with Albertsons. "They should bring diverse viewpoints, perspectives, and experiences." Amanda, who has always worked in operations, has sought out mentors with other areas of expertise, such as human resources and retail. "The feedback I get from them is always surprising because they see the world differently than I do," she says.

To find a mentor, start by identifying a role model: someone who inspires you. Let the person know something you admire about her or him. Who doesn't love a compliment? Then request a 30-minute meeting to go over some career-related questions. If that conversation goes well, ask to schedule a regular check-in. If the answer is yes, you've found yourself a mentor. From there, take responsibility for owning and directing the relationship. Set the agenda, and ask great questions. Complete your agreed-upon tasks.

Here's a common scenario: You approached someone you admire, boldly asked that person to mentor you, and got a "yes." But a year into the relationship, those conversations don't invigorate you the way they used to, and you suspect they aren't as energizing for your mentor either. Don't be too quick to write off the relationship. Sometimes it's not the relationship that's stale—you just need fresh material to discuss. It's possible to reinvigorate your mentoring sessions by bringing a thoughtful, diverse slate of questions.

Four Types of Questions to Ask a Mentor

Here are four types of questions to ask your mentor: stories, situations, self-awareness, and skill building. Take one of each type to every mentoring conversation to keep things interesting—and valuable—for both of you.

Mentor Question Type 1. Stories

To kick-start the conversation, ask your mentor to tell a story from his or her own career. You could ask, "How did you get to where you are today?" or "How did you land in your current role?"

But you could also ask more specific questions, such as these, to get to the heart of your career objectives and concerns:

- Was there a time you messed up and felt like you'd failed? What did you do to recover?
- How did you learn to embrace risk taking?
- How did you become such a polished presenter?
- Which were the leadership skills you worked hardest to develop?
- Think back to five years ago. Did you envision this is where you would be?

Mentor Question Type 2. Situations

Now that the conversation is flowing, you can bring a specific situation to your mentor that you'd like help navigating. For example:

- I tried to delegate a task last week, and it did not go as well as I'd expected. Can we work through what to do differently next time?
- Who are the people I need to align with in this organization to be successful?
- My boss said I need to be more strategic. What does that mean?
- How can I let my boss know that I don't need to be micromanaged?
- What should I include in a proposal to convince my manager to greenlight a stretch assignment?

Mentor Question Type 3. Self-Awareness

One of the greatest strengths you can develop for yourself is the gift of self-awareness, meaning the ability to see yourself as others view you. A mentor's feedback can help you develop the strong internal compass for insightful and accurate self-evaluation that I mentioned in Chapter 2.

With self-awareness, you'll know when to strengthen an already positive perception, or when it's necessary to take steps to change any negative perceptions others have of you. Your mentor can assist by "holding up the mirror" and providing detailed feedback on how others see you. Ask questions such as these:

- How am I viewed—that is, what's my personal brand—in our organization?
- Where do you see my leadership strengths?
- What do you see as some of my blind spots?
- Do I come across as strategic or tactical in my day-to-day communication?
- How do people describe me when I'm not in the room?

Mentor Question Type 4. Skill Building

Is there a skill you're currently working to enhance? Ask your mentor for advice and resources that will help you polish that skill, with questions like these:

- How can I become better at influencing people who do not report to me?
- Can we role-play asking for a promotion and raise?
- Do you have any quick tips for reenergizing an overworked team?
- Can you recommend a book or resource for dealing with difficult conversations?
- Do you have a template you use for developing a long-range vision and strategic plan?

Find more examples of questions at www.jomiller.com/mentor.

With these four types of questions, you'll never need to sit through another mentoring conversation wondering if the other person is finding the discussion interesting. So rather than add a new mentor to your network, here's a different challenge: reinvigorate an existing mentorship by preparing thoughtfully for each discussion.

OWN IT

Four Types of Questions to Ask a Mentor

- Schedule your next check-in with a mentor, and prepare by creating one question from each of the four types (stories, situations, self-awareness, and skill building).
- Share the list of four types of questions with the people you mentor, and ask them to direct future conversations.

MOBILIZE YOUR INNER CIRCLE

Ask yourself, "Whom am I surrounding myself with, and are they bringing out the best in me?"

For a well-rounded, supportive network, include least one of each of the four types (connector, informational powerhouse, influencer, and mentor) in your core crew of associates. Whether your objective is to advance your career, make a course correction, lead a major project, transform an organization, or make any type of bold, fearless move, having a diverse and influential inner circle makes the journey easier.

In a like-attracts-like business world where women are outnumbered in senior leadership ranks, we often have to work harder to develop the relationships that make up our networks, but it is through these connections that we blossom most as leaders and draw empowerment to make an even bigger difference in the areas we care about.

Don't shortchange yourself by playing it safe. Instead, take some risks, and reach out to some people you admire. They'll benefit from knowing you, too, with the enthusiasm and passion you bring for the unique niche you serve and the "go big or go home" impact you're out to create.

OWN IT

Four People You Need in Your Network

- Review your close contacts to see if you have at least one person from each category: connector, informational powerhouse, influencer, and mentor.
- Think of whom you'd like to include in your support squad, and add them to your networking plan.

OUTSOURCE IT

Four People You Need in Your Network

- If you know a great connector who trusts you and believes in you, share the list of four types of people with her or him, along with your lofty goal. Ask if there's anyone she or he would recommend you get to know.

CHAPTER 8 WRAP-UP

In this chapter, you took a closer look at your most precious asset, your network, and ways make it even more valuable. Developing these bonds is not optional: it is the real work of leadership.

"People do not follow a title," says Dara Bazzano, chief accounting officer with CBRE. "They follow a person whom they trust, respect, and believe in. Somebody they know has got their back."

You might not become friends with everyone you work with, but you can certainly gain their trust. Without that, you'll only place limits on yourself.

You won't avoid office politics, so don't even try. Instead, engage your curiosity, become a student of social dynamics, and develop your positive political skill. With your shadow organization map, strategic networking plan, and four key people to include in your network, you can develop a strong community, and that will make you a stronger leader. Oh, and even enhance your well-being and health.

There's one more person you need in your support squad, and that person's presence can completely transform your career. Who this person is and how to find her or him is the sole focus of Chapter 9.

9

Attract Influential Advocates

Enlist Support to Kick Down Doors

> One of the best things you can do
> for yourself is to become an asset to
> someone you aspire to be like.
> **—Sandra Veszi Einhorn,**
> executive director,
> Coordinating Council of Broward

Early in her career, Cindy Kent had an inkling that her work as a manufacturing engineer was not her life's calling. "I couldn't find myself getting very passionate about that work," says Cindy. She was interested in looking for a different role, but very quickly she ran into a brick wall.

That wall was a company policy. Cindy's employer, a pharmaceutical company, was running an FDA-regulated manufacturing operation, and it had estimated that it took five years to recoup its investment in training a new engineer. A policy was put in place requiring engineers like Cindy to stay in their roles for five years before being eligible to move to a new one.

But the job didn't fully engage her. She knew she just could not do it.

Meanwhile, Cindy had been volunteering for an employee resource group when its executive sponsor, a vice president for operations in a different area of the business, invited Cindy to lunch and told her he liked her energy, passion, and commitment to the employee group. He asked what she wanted to do next. Says Cindy, "I wasn't sure because I had not been exposed to much else." So the executive offered to pay for her to take a battery of talent development assessments to help figure it out.

Almost immediately, things started happening, but behind the scenes in ways that were invisible to Cindy. Later, she learned that the vice president had challenged her management, saying, "I'd much rather break our own rule than lose her to another company that recognizes her talent."

Within six months, Cindy received the green light to move into sales, which had been identified as one of her potential areas of strength. From there, her career took off. "It opened up so many leadership opportunities. I honestly believe that my entire career trajectory changed as a result of being able to learn about commercial operations and sales so early in my career," says Cindy, who now sits on Best Buy's board of directors. And it might not have happened that way if not for that lunchtime conversation.

Like many first-time protégés, it was only with hindsight that Cindy became aware of what sponsorship is and the extent to which her sponsor had advocated for her. "I didn't call it 'sponsorship' at that time. But now, as I reflect back on it, I recognize that that was exactly what it was," she says.

SO WHAT IS A SPONSOR, EXACTLY?

If there's a brick wall standing between you and your next career breakthrough (or if you'd like to act preemptively to avoid future walls), having a sponsor can make an enormous difference. But because sponsors are less understood and less utilized than mentors, but equally important, I have devoted this entire chapter to sponsorship. I'll cover what sponsorship is, how it works, how it differs from mentorship, and techniques for attracting your own influential advocates.

So, what is a sponsor, exactly? I asked three leaders to define sponsorship, based on their own experience. Here are their responses:

- "A sponsor is an influential spokesperson for what you are capable of doing," said Millette Granville, vice president, talent, diversity and inclusion, and organizational development for Food Lion.

- "Sponsors use their internal political and social capital to move your career forward within an organization. Behind closed doors, they will argue your case," said Cindy Kent.
- "A sponsor is a person with a seat at the decision-making table who will throw your name out for coveted assignments and promotion opportunities," said Amanda Martinez, group vice president of corporate procurement with Albertsons Companies.

Sponsors are capable of spotting strengths you're not even aware of yet because they are underdeveloped. They see how your strengths could add value in areas of the business you've not yet been exposed to. The best sponsors can see a vision for your career that is bigger than you could ever imagine. And if you're ready to break through to your next great career challenge, you won't have to kick down doors on your own. Due to their influence, sponsors can open more doors than you ever thought possible.

Having a sponsor is also like navigating your career wrapped in an extra-thick layer of bubble wrap. Sponsors can protect you during organizational shake-ups, such as acquisitions, reorgs, or layoffs, and mitigate the downsides of making bolder, riskier career moves. And it's not an exaggeration to say that with one sponsor's advocacy, your career can find a new trajectory for you to catapult forward.

THE DIFFERENCE BETWEEN MENTORS AND SPONSORS

I first learned about sponsorship when an article titled "Why Men Still Get More Promotions Than Women" appeared in the *Harvard Business Review*.[1] The title alone was a real attention-grabber.

Here's the part that stuck in my mind: "There is a special kind of relationship—called sponsorship—in which the mentor goes beyond giving feedback and advice and uses her or his influence with senior executives to advocate for the mentee," wrote Herminia Ibarra, Nancy M. Carter, and Christine Silva. Their interviews and surveys had suggested that high-potential women are *overmentored* and *undersponsored* relative to their male peers—a significant reason women were not advancing as rapidly.

MISSTEP 11

Let me repeat for emphasis: *being overmentored and undersponsored* is Misstep 11.

Despite what you read, if you want to advance your career, it's not enough to have mentors. Don't get me wrong: mentors are truly wonderful people. They help you gain critical skills, guide you through everyday challenges at work, and offer a sounding board when you're at a career crossroads. But if you aspire to climb and gain influence, you need sponsors too. That's why the Leaderly Move is *attracting the advocacy of influential sponsors.*

To articulate the difference between a mentor and a sponsor, I turned to women leaders who have been exceptional in both roles:

- "Mentors give you perspective, while sponsors give you opportunities," said Cate Huston, engineering lead with Automattic.
- "A mentor will talk with you, but a sponsor will talk about you," said Heather Foust-Cummings, senior vice president, research and consulting, with Catalyst, a nonprofit that conducts research into women's advancement.[2]
  - To which I will add: mentors help you skill up whereas sponsors help you move up.

> Mentors help you skill up whereas sponsors help you move up.

OWN IT

The Difference Between Mentors and Sponsors

Think about the different roles played by mentors and sponsors. Which type of support are you most in need of right now?

The Help You Don't Know You Need

Among the preworkshop surveys I analyzed, sponsorship was a blind spot, or at least the word "sponsor" was. Only 3 out of 1,200 participants who completed the survey mentioned wanting to develop, or expand, sponsorships. When I took a closer look, I discovered many felt tapped out on their efforts to advance on their own. Some recognized that an influential advocate could help but hadn't found one yet. Here are some of the responses:

- I struggle with getting access to the next great role.
- I don't feel like I have someone looking out for me.
- My greatest challenge is getting the right people to believe in me and bet on me so I can move on to new levels.
- I want decision makers to think of me when it comes to promotions.
- I am looking for tips on how to network with more senior people and gain visibility for my work.

Others were confounded by having a clear goal but seeing no clear path to reach it. "Getting to director level is a mystery," declared one. "I have worked really hard to perform at the next level to get a promotion but am still not getting it. Now I feel stuck," said another. Others shared their frustration with not finding opportunities to grow and learn or switch to a better-suited role.

Rereading their responses, I wanted to reach back and assure them that it's OK to ask for help, and it's OK to accept help. You don't need to face down these obstacles alone. My Be Leaderly colleague Selena Rezvani likens a sponsor to rocket fuel for your career. Whether you're struggling to lift off the launch pad, or attempting to alter the trajectory or velocity of your ascent, a sponsor's help is invaluable.

To truly grasp the impact of sponsorship and the boost in momentum it can add to your career, here are facts worth knowing:

- **There's a sponsorship gap.** Women are less likely than their male peers to benefit from sponsorship, according to Sylvia Ann Hewlett and her coauthors of *The Sponsor Effect: Breaking Through the Last Glass Ceiling.* Only 13 percent of women versus

19 percent of men working full time for large companies have a sponsor.[3] That gender gap may be smaller than you'd have guessed, but it's still significant—and it has a cascading effect. Without sponsorship, you're less likely to advance. That gender gap is one of the reasons men still outnumber women nearly two to one in top leadership positions. The race gap is wider still. Only 8 percent of people of color have a sponsor.[4]

- **Sponsors empower you to make bold moves.** People who have the backing of a powerful sponsor are at least 22 percent more likely to summon the courage to ask for stretch assignments and raises.[5] A sponsor provides a career safety net, and that makes it easier to be bolder, take risks, and ask for what you want. This matters a lot because people who ask for a raise, promotion, or job change are far more likely to receive it than those who don't.[6]

- **Sponsors enhance career satisfaction.** How happy are you, right now, with the pace of your career growth? Women and men feel more satisfied with their career advancement when they have sponsors.[7] If you feel like your career has plateaued or that you're being overlooked for opportunities, a sponsor can jump-start your momentum.

- **Sponsors transfer a "halo" of power to protégés.** "Four U.S.-based and global studies clearly show that sponsorship—not mentorship—is how power is transferred in the workplace," reported Jenna Goodreau for *Business Insider*.[8] If women are less likely to be sponsored than their male colleagues, then it's no surprise that it's more difficult for women to gain influence. Whether you're aiming to launch a new product, turn around a struggling team, or attract broader responsibilities, having an influential ally in your corner makes life easier.

- **You're underestimating the benefits of sponsorship.** Here's one final nugget of information from the research referenced in *The Sponsor Effect*. Wrote the authors, "We found that the majority of ambitious women underestimate the pivotal role sponsorship plays in their advancement—not just within their current firm, but throughout their career and across their industry."

The surveys of my workshop attendees certainly support that finding. While 76 percent felt their direct manager knew of their accomplishments and strengths, only half said their boss's boss did. And the gap widened when it came to sharing their aspirations. Fully 60 percent said their manager was aware of their career goals, but only 29 percent said the manager up one more level knew their goals. With their achievements and aspirations going unrecognized by leaders in such close proximity, just one level removed from their own manager, no wonder these women felt that their next great role or career-accelerating assignment was elusive.

When I'm delivering a workshop or keynote about sponsorship, I like to ask, "Have *you* ever had a sponsor?" It's typical for less than 20 percent of the group to raise their hands. So, I rephrase the question, "Raise your hand if you suspect you may have had a sponsor, with 75 percent or greater certainty." With that prompt, I will see a ripple of realization move across the room, resulting in a show of hands from about a third of the group. My point is that it's not always entirely clear when sponsorship is in play. Sometimes it requires a moment of reflection to identify that you have indeed had a sponsor. Frequently, as in Cindy Kent's experience, sponsorship is invisible to us.

WORKING WITH
MENTORS AND SPONSORS

While you'll always benefit from receiving input from mentors and sponsors, people typically utilize them differently during different career phases. If you're just starting out, enlist the support of mentors to help you identify strengths to focus on as you lay down an early track record of achievement. Sponsorship generally kicks in once you've established a baseline of great performance and have some ideas for where you'd like to go next.

It's to your benefit to be candid in conversations with mentors, but less so with sponsors. I asked Amanda Martinez for her take on the differences between the two roles. "A mentor is somebody with whom you can talk through something that's a real challenge where you're not quite sure what to do," Amanda said. Those aren't situations you want to work through with a sponsor. "You want your sponsor to focus on what makes you different and better than your competition for a coveted role," she said. Sponsors need to be able to speak of your strengths, your accomplishments, and what you're working toward. They don't need to know how difficult an accomplishment was, she added.

It's not uncommon to find yourself in a situation in which one person is fulfilling both roles. If that happens to you, be selective in the mentoring questions you ask them, and find other mentors for support when you're working through a weakness or a difficult challenge.

What's in It for the Sponsor

Long before Sallie Krawcheck held CEO roles at Citi and Merrill Lynch, back when she was a research analyst, a more senior colleague took an interest in her work. He read her research, corrected it, and offered insightful critiques. He coached her on presentations, talked her up to clients, and advocated for Sallie to receive promotions. And when his recommendations were not acted on, he took it up with management.

"This cut years off of my career trajectory," says Sallie, now CEO of Ellevest and chair of Pax Ellevate.[9] "I could compare myself to equally smart, hardworking colleagues who started at about the same time I did but were a couple of years behind in their success."

The advocacy can flow in both directions. In time, Sallie was reading her senior colleague's research, making suggestions, and recommending him to her clients. It evolved into being much more of a reciprocal relationship than sponsorship is typically understood to be. A successful sponsorship relationship will benefit the sponsor too. "We don't talk about that mutual benefit enough," says Sallie.

If you're talented and hardworking and your sponsor helps you land where you shine, it's seen as a smart move on a sponsor's part. A leader who makes a series of successful bets on people's potential versus a proven track record often becomes known as a talent scout and developer, which in turn tends to attract engaged followers. That makes it easier for this type of sponsor to build teams from scratch, quickly staff up a department or even a whole organization, and attract and retain the crème de la crème in a competitive market or industry.

So don't ever feel like the sponsorship relationship is one-way. It's not. By advocating for others, a sponsor stands out too, particularly in contrast to managers who feel threatened by a rising star (or even try to squelch their prospects). Sponsors set themselves apart by showing that they're the type of leaders who cultivate other leaders and derive satisfaction from helping others succeed. If you ask me, that's one of the most revealing characteristics that separates the true leaders from the wannabes. You don't have to be a manager or executive to enjoy the benefits of sponsoring others. Training yourself to recognize the strengths in others and connecting them to stretch opportunities is a great way to prove your leadership chops. Later in this chapter, I'll recommend some ways to do that.

Sponsorship Is Rarely Requested, Always Earned

"OK," I hear you thinking. "How do I get a sponsor?" How do you, as a newer or unproven leader, build a case for a potential sponsor to speak up, put you forward for a coveted role, and invest their hefty career capital on your behalf?

Not so fast. Keep in mind that sponsorship, like trust, is something you earn. Whatever you do, don't try to initiate a relationship by asking, "Will you sponsor me?" When people sponsor you, they put their own reputation at risk. They first need to understand your body of work, who you are, and how you present yourself.

"How do you get a sponsor?" I asked Cindy Kent and Amanda Martinez as we prepared for a webinar on the topic. They responded, almost in unison, that that's not how sponsorship works. "It's not the up-and-comer choosing the sponsor," explained Amanda.

You don't choose the sponsor. The sponsor chooses you.

Think about it. Sponsors need to trust that you'll represent them well and you'll do what's best for the business. Before recommending you for a larger role or a business-critical project, they need to understand your strengths and untapped potential. And they need to have faith that you'll deliver. They also need

> **You don't choose the sponsor. The sponsor chooses you.**

to know enough about your preferences to be sure you'll say yes to an assignment before they talk you up. This level of trust can only be built over time.

Sponsorship is not a relationship that is built in the time it takes to ask, "Hey, Sallie, will you sponsor me?" during a drive-by hallway conversation. Asking for sponsorship outright can get awkward and even backfire.

Sponsorship grows organically, without being discussed or forced. "I have never asked 'Would you be my sponsor?'" says Sallie Krawcheck. She cringes at the thought. If your plan is to catch someone off guard like that, be prepared to hear, "What the heck's a sponsor?" or worse.

Sallie's experience is a case in point. "One moment, he was answering my question in a mentoring conversation. Then, all of a sudden, he was fighting for me, and telling others 'Here is a talented and hardworking individual,'" she says.

FIVE BEHAVIORS FOR ATTRACTING SPONSORS

In its report titled *Sponsoring Women to Success*, Catalyst flat out stated "There is no 'silver bullet' for attracting the attention of a high-level sponsor."

However, through my years of coaching emerging leaders and interviewing sponsors and protégés about how sponsorship is earned, I have identified five behaviors that you can adopt to swing the odds in your favor. We'll take a look at each in detail:

Behavior 1. Learn to spot sponsors.

Behavior 2. Establish credibility.

Behavior 3. Raise your hand for exposure opportunities.

Behavior 4. Have clear, courageous career goals.

Behavior 5. Share your goals with leaders.

Behavior 1. Learn to Spot Sponsors

If your company is like most, there will be a limited number of people in your organization or industry who have both the desire and the influence to act as sponsors. So how will you know potential sponsors when you see them? They'll show up as *talent spotters* who are *respected* and *influential*. Those are the leaders you want on your side. Let's take a closer look at these three characteristics.

Respected

It's essential that your sponsor is someone you and others respect. Pay attention to leaders who have earned the trust of their peers and superiors. Look for those whose values and ethics are in line with your own and with those of the organization. Ideally, sponsors are widely respected by others such that when they speak on your behalf, their recommendation will carry weight.

In return, be prepared to stand by your sponsor. In an interview with *Business Insider*, Sylvia Ann Hewlett, author of *Forget a Mentor, Find a Sponsor: The New Way to Fast-Track Your Career*, points out that sponsors benefit when you contribute a unique, indispensable skill set and deliver outstanding results.[10] But what sponsors value above all is your loyalty.

"Star performers are very likely to attract sponsors, and loyal performers are very likely to keep them," says Sylvia Ann. Think about it: if someone is willing to stick her or his neck out to support you, the worst thing you can do is to break that trust. So ask yourself, "Can I be unconditionally loyal to this person?"

Sponsorship also entails aligning your career prospects with those of your sponsor. If your sponsor leaves or is disenfranchised, you, as a rising star, might crash back down to earth.

Influential

If sponsors are going to open doors for you and connect you with new opportunities, their word must carry authority. They must have influence. Says Amanda Martinez, "Sponsors are people who will nominate you, speak of your strengths, and get you those assignments that are sought after. They'll also give you exposure to key leaders that you might not otherwise have exposure to."

An ideal sponsor is one who can introduce you to an overscheduled, high-ranking leader and successfully make the case that it's worth making time to meet with you. Good sponsors have the chops to persuade their peers that the risk of losing you to an outside opportunity outweighs the consequences of breaking a company policy. They can convincingly recommend you as a quick study, capable of succeeding in a role that's outside your experience. When an effective sponsor speaks, people listen. And don't overlook your peers as potential sponsors, if they have those qualities. As Millette Granville points out, "A sponsor does not have to be an executive but does need to have influence."

A Talent Spotter

Most important, a sponsor is someone who is willing to place a bet on untapped potential and as-yet-unproven talent.

At a time in her career when she was working in human resources, Cindy Kent developed an interest in marketing. Her sponsor at the time was her senior vice president, who knew how well Cindy was delivering in her role. While it would have been in his personal best interests to keep her in HR, Cindy's sponsor was able to look beyond her immediate utility and envision her future path. He said, "I believe in her talent. We want to see her operating at the highest levels of leadership." In an unprecedented move, he allowed her to work in marketing for a year while keeping her headcount and salary in his HR group. Of the qualities that make a great sponsor, Cindy says, "They're willing to do something unconventional to advocate for you."

A seasoned sponsor will have an established history of spotting and cultivating talent. Look for people whose success you'd like to emulate, and then trace a path back to their sponsors. "Your sponsor needs to be someone whom people see as a good judge of performance," Amanda says. "That makes his or her vote much more powerful."

If you're not familiar with the active sponsors in your organization, it's time you find out. Here's how:

- Look for leaders who publicly praise subordinates, back them up on contentious issues, and offer challenging assignments to unproven up-and-comers.
- Ask around to discover which leaders have hands-on involvement with talent development initiatives, such as mentoring and high-potential programs.
- Observe the career paths of emerging leaders among your peers, and see if you can figure out who is sponsoring them.

If someone's career seems to be taking off, chances are there's a sponsor or two behind the scenes, facilitating that advancement.

- Attend employee resource group events to see which executive sponsors and speakers are the most involved and committed.
- Pay attention when colleagues speak highly of the boss who made a big difference in their career or entrusted them with an assignment that broadened their capabilities or raised their profile.
- When an emerging leader speaks up in a meeting, notice who supports her, endorses her ideas, and backs up her decisions.
- When your organization encounters turbulence, like downsizing, reorgs, or leadership changes, watch out for leaders who are protecting protégés from the negative impacts.

Also look for potential sponsors beyond your immediate work group. Having advocates outside your direct management chain can reduce your vulnerability during layoffs or reorgs. "Get to know individuals at other companies as well," says Sallie Krawcheck, pointing out the limitation of a network that stops at your office door. She continues, "You can have sponsors who are not within your own company, and they can be very powerful in getting you onto boards and advisory committees."

OWN IT

Learn to Spot Sponsors

Make a list of leaders in your organization and/or industry who are respected, influential talent spotters.

OUTSOURCE IT

Learn to Spot Sponsors

If you have friends or colleagues in your organization whose careers have taken off, ask if they are aware of who is sponsoring them.

Behavior 2. Establish Credibility

To understand what sponsors need from you, it's helpful to consider what they're categorically *not* looking for. Says Sallie, "If you are not committed to your job, if you don't deliver your work on time, if you leave on Fridays at two o'clock and say, 'I'm working from home' when everybody knows you're not, then nobody is going to want to sponsor you."

You already know this, but I'll underscore it: great performance is essential. Convincing a potential sponsor that you're worth taking a risk on starts with doing great work. It's premature to expect a sponsor to recommend you for your next role if you haven't yet delivered outstanding performance in your current one.

Prior to founding Kokko, Nina Bhatti was chief performance architect for HP, one of the company's highest-ranked technical women, and her research resulted in commercially successful products for some of HP's largest customers. Nina is also an example of how to deliver the level of performance that leads to sponsorship—even in the early years of your career. I asked Nina about her journey to establishing the type of record that sponsors are on the lookout for.

To begin, says Nina, be aware that you're being observed. People will be watching to see if you can be relied on to deliver what you say you'll deliver. "Your first job is to build credibility. I don't think there is anything more important than that," she says. When given an assignment, execute it well. Show confidence, enthusiasm, and professionalism, and people will learn to trust you. "Train people that you are good for it, and that you can be relied on to deliver," Nina emphasized.

How will you know when you've gained credibility? For Nina, that confirmation arrived the day a manager threw her a large, intimidating, and ambiguous assignment. She says, "I was overwhelmed. It was truly scary." Nina asked her manager, "What do you want me to do?" Her manager replied, "I don't know. I am not going to tell you how to do your job. Something good will happen that wasn't going to happen without you."

"See how much trust I had built with him?" says Nina. She went on to figure out for herself what was required and how to measure the project's success, and then she executed the assignment. She learned the skill of walking into the unknown and managing herself.

When it comes to building credibility, Nina's advice is to go above and beyond in your role, contribute to your organization's goals, and contribute like a rock star. "Never forget what your main goal is," she says.

Behavior 3. Raise Your Hand for Exposure Opportunities

Sponsors have finely honed instincts for identifying strengths—ones that may be underdeveloped, that their owner might not even be aware of.

Sponsorship begins when someone spots talent in an up-and-comer, explains Amanda Martinez. In Amanda's case, a sponsor reached out to show interest in helping her, saying, "I think you would be a fantastic candidate for this role."

The role turned out to be in a completely different part of the organization—one that Amanda would not otherwise have considered. When the sponsor described why this would be good for her career, Amanda made a leap of faith. She moved out of inventory management and into distribution and transportation. "I might have been fearful of failing, but my sponsor strongly encouraged me to take the job," says Amanda. Her success in the role resulted in a remarkably different path and dramatically accelerated her career.

Before sponsors can facilitate such leaps, they need to become familiar with your work. If they get questioned or challenged about their decision to promote you, they'll need evidence, based on their experience. If you keep your head down and stay in your cube, your performance won't be apparent to them. "Exposure is a foundational building block for sponsorship and for career advancement," says Cindy Kent. "Find opportunities for people to catch you at your best doing your best work."

Whatever you do, *don't be the best-kept secret in the organization.* This, as you know, is one of my signature mantras. If you want a sponsor to believe in you, encourage you, and throw you into situations in which you'll develop and grow, you need to make your strengths and accomplishments visible, as described in Chapter 7.

Would you expect a sponsor to go out on a limb to endorse you without knowing the quality of your work and what you're capable of? Of course not. Raise your hand for exposure opportunities to work with or for potential sponsors, where your performance will be clearly apparent.

This could mean looking for a stretch assignment, like the ones described in Chapter 6, working directly for a leader who has the qualities of a potential sponsor. Your goal is for that leader to see you in action and directly experience the highest quality of work you can deliver.

Nina Bhatti recommends finding an initiative that you want to work on and that is on a leader's goal list. "The sponsor needs to have something to gain from your success," says Nina. "Look for someone whose objectives are in alignment with what you want to do."

Early in Nina's career, after establishing credibility in her role, she approached a senior vice president who needed to accomplish something for a large customer. "I showed him something that I could do that he really needed to deliver," she recalls. As a result, the senior vice president was intrinsically motivated to become her sponsor.

Behavior 4. Have Clear, Courageous Career Goals

I once coached Alex, a project manager, who had taken what appeared to be a big step backward in her career. Formerly the manager of a large team, whom she had led through a transformation initiative, she had been hired by her new employer as an individual contributor, to manage some process improvements. At first, Alex didn't see that as a setback. She had identified her new employer as one she wanted to spend the rest of her career with, and she figured she would quickly recover the lost ground. But a year into her new role, she was beginning to have second thoughts. I asked whether her leaders were aware of her goal to move back into management. Alex said she was not certain they were.

Together, Alex and I came up with a plan. Over the next two weeks, she would make her goal known to five leaders—at moments when it seemed appropriate.

Alex admitted that this seemed daunting, so we worked together on what she would say and came up with the script: "I believe I have mastered my current role, and I'm interested in moving back into a management position where I can drive process excellence." We role-played a couple times until she felt prepared.

Later the same day, one of Alex's leaders stopped by to check in on progress related to her project. As their conversation was wrapping up and he turned to leave, Alex said "Wait, there's one more thing." Despite feeling a knot in her stomach, she repeated her script. The leader nodded and left, as though Alex's words had not sunk in. But later that day he returned, saying "I might have just the opportunity for you." His offer: to relocate within the company and manage a large team. She accepted, and the move served her well. Within two years, she had leapfrogged into a director-level role, where she's been highly effective.

Caveat: I'm by no means guaranteeing that you'll attract an influential advocate this rapidly. That's *not* the point of this story. The point is this: a sponsor won't know what opportunities to match you with if you don't know what you want for yourself. Take away the guesswork by identifying your career goals and crisply, memorably, and repeatedly articulating what you want.

And, as a reminder, a sponsor is like rocket fuel for your career. If your destination is a two-block walk from your current location, it would be unwise to expend spacecraft propellant to get there. Make no small plans. Instead, have lofty goals (like the one you identified in Chapter 2) and sponsor-worthy aspirations of where you'd like to boldly go. Have a destination in mind that's distinct *and* daring.

> **Make no small plans. Instead, have lofty goals and sponsor-worthy aspirations of where you'd like to boldly go.**

Behavior 5. Share Your Goals with Leaders

Once you have laid the groundwork by identifying potential sponsors, building credibility, taking on assignments that made your performance apparent, and setting clear, courageous career goals, the final step in securing sponsorship is a relatively simple one: sharing your goals with potential sponsors.

"It was not until fairly recently that I realized that I truly am in the driver's seat in my career," says Amanda Martinez, who saw that she needed to initiate those conversations and do it with leaders throughout her company. If you don't tell them what you're interested in, they'll never know to think of you when those openings occur. "You might be uncomfortable doing that the first time, but it gets easier," says Amanda. The people whose help you want will often be willing, but you have to have the courage to speak up.

By articulating and reiterating what you want to do, you can make a leader's life easier the next time there's a role to fill, a special project to assign, or a team to staff up. And once you've earned their respect, communicating your aspirations with your manager, your mentors, and other leaders in your upper-management chain (and beyond) can often be enough to enlist their sponsorship.

OWN IT

Five Behaviors for Attracting Sponsors

Review the five behaviors for attracting a sponsor's advocacy and identify one to work on.

OUTSOURCE IT

Five Behaviors for Attracting Sponsors

If you have mentors and managers whom you've established credibility with, share your career goal with them.

PAY IT FORWARD

No one makes this climb alone.

Those of us who have had any level of success in our careers are here because of our merits *and* because of our sponsors. Someone spotted a strength that was unproven or not fully formed, or bragged about our talent. Someone threw our name into the ring for a stretch role or assignment—or even *created* that role or assignment. We are sponsorship trophies: someone gets to point to us and feel a tremendous sense of achievement.

MISSTEP 12

We've all worked with people so gripped by ambition that they climbed over others to get ahead. I've heard them described as the types who "kiss up and kick down." *Climbing the ladder and then kicking it away* (or worse, letting it land on someone) is the final misstep. The Leaderly Move is *lifting others up as you rise.*

Remember, you don't have to be an executive to enjoy the reward and satisfaction of being someone's sponsor. If you've accrued social capital and influence, use them to advocate for others. Hone your talent-spotting instincts by paying attention to the strengths of your peers, especially the hidden gems who are being underutilized. Get to know their aspirations. Stick your neck out and become their visible and vocal advocate, especially when it comes to roles or assignments that would be a stretch. In doing so, you'll also mark yourself as a leader and become more sponsorship savvy. But be aware that sponsorship is *not* favoritism, at least not when it's done right. We need to recognize and correct for our own biases.

We typically think of sponsorship in terms of large gestures, like helping someone land the right job. But smaller, everyday actions can be real difference makers too. "Micro-sponsorships are small acts of support and advocacy that take place in the moment," says Caroline Simard, PhD, managing director of the Stanford VMware Women's Leadership Innovation Lab, where she leads research efforts to advance women's leadership.

Caroline recommends looking for opportunities such as speaking up to affirm a person's competency, calling attention to a key contribution, or correcting the record when someone's idea is attributed to someone else. Micro-sponsoring peers can also involve bringing their name up for a desirable assignment or facilitating a valuable networking connection. According to Caroline, these acts of micro-sponsorship can also be a way to model inclusive behavior and push back at bias—that is, when individuals are singled out or overlooked on the basis of their race, gender, or other differences.

Here's an important truthbomb: *sponsorship begets sponsorship*. People who have been sponsored pay it forward.[11] They are more likely to be sponsors themselves, and they are more likely to develop other engaged and committed leaders. This is especially true of women and minorities. Diverse talent pays it forward by sponsoring diverse talent.

If you've progressed beyond midlevel, you've gotten to where you are as the beneficiary of mentorship and sponsorship, and you're likely starting to "give back" by mentoring and sponsoring others. But are you contributing to a *culture* of sponsorship?

If you have clout in your organization, there are tangible ways you can make a difference to closing the gender and race sponsorship gaps. Be open about what it would take for you to sponsor someone. Talk to other leaders about what sponsorship is and why it matters. Be a champion for reevaluating who gets identified as high potential, ensuring diverse talent isn't overlooked, and matching participants to sponsors.

Power doesn't just randomly trickle down through layers of an organization. It is channeled deliberately via sponsorship. Bring sponsorship out from behind closed doors, so it becomes more open, transparent, and equitable.

OWN IT

Pay It Forward

Use your social capital to sponsor others:
- If you're early in your career, use micro-sponsorship with a small act of support or advocacy.
- If you're midlevel, find an opportunity to recommend someone for a stretch role or assignment.
- If you're senior level, think of a way to use your influence to contribute to an equitable culture of sponsorship, and act on it.

CHAPTER 9 WRAP-UP

If you've been looking for a missing, mysterious career-enhancing *x* factor, it might just be sponsorship.

Sponsors lay their personal, political, and social capital on the line to advocate on your behalf. They spot strengths you aren't yet aware of, see a bigger vision for your future, and have the influence to move your career forward.

Although sponsorship can be like rocket fuel for your career, it isn't something you just ask for. You earn the right, by doing your homework, identifying potential sponsors, and making your credibility, value, and aspirations known.

You don't have to make this climb alone. With influential advocates you can bust through walls and kick open doors together.

Conclusion
Leave a Lasting Leadership Legacy

> *We are the leaders we've been looking for.*
> **—Grace Lee Boggs,**
> author, philosopher, and activist

Thank you for sticking with me this far. You should be proud of yourself: you've now got the tools and to-dos to thrive as a rising woman of influence and become the leader you were meant to be. To recap, here are the nine chapters that we've worked so hard through together:

Chapter 1. Put on Your Big Girl Pants: Lead from Where You Are

Chapter 2. You Do You: Own Your Leadership Strengths

Chapter 3. What's Your Superpower? Claim Your Leadership Niche

Chapter 4. Boss Up Your Brand: Up-Level How You're Perceived

Chapter 5. Get Your Shift Together: Shift Your Mindset from Doing to Leading

Chapter 6. Go Big or Go Home: Create Career-Defining Moments

Chapter 7. Amplify Your Accomplishments: Don't Be the Best-Kept Secret

Chapter 8. Rally Your Crew: The Four People You Need in Your Corner

Chapter 9. Attract Influential Advocates: Enlist Support to Kick Down Doors

Author, social activist, and philosopher Grace Lee Boggs was asked at age 91 to name leaders who were societal change makers. Instead of answering the question, she called for a new definition of leadership. "I think we need to embrace the idea that we are the leaders we've been looking for," said Boggs.[1]

You're already a leader in your own right, whether you're leading projects, initiatives, teams, or an organization. The beauty of expanding your influence is there's a whole new level of impact you get to make. As you consider how you'll use that influence, I have a few final suggestions.

THANK YOUR MENTORS AND SPONSORS

I've had incredible mentors and sponsors who have guided me through tough career decisions, boosted my skills, given me an infusion of confidence, and thrown me into big, exciting, scary opportunities. No doubt you've had wonderful advocates and champions too. How can you possibly thank them for all they've done and all they mean to you?

There's the time-honored, handwritten thank-you note and modern-day LinkedIn testimonial. You can treat for lunch or an after-work celebratory cocktail. All of these are good.

But here's something they might appreciate even more.

A number of years ago, I listened to an executive panel at a women's leadership conference sponsored by a Fortune 500 company. An audience member asked, "How can I thank my mentor?" The execs' response was unanimous: Pay it forward by mentoring someone else.

Yes, your mentors and sponsors gain immense satisfaction from seeing your growth and success. But they also do what they do out of a deep sense of service, motivated in part by gratitude to someone who believed in them, encouraged them, and helped them become all that they are today.

By investing in others, in turn, you honor those who invested in you.

So thank your mentors, sponsors, collaborators, and coopetition by letting them know that they've inspired you to mentor, sponsor, assist, accelerate, support, or encourage someone else. I guarantee this will make their day. Plus, it's the right thing to do.

LIFT OTHERS AS YOU RISE

Stepping up as a leader can feel risky. You're testing out new skills, sharing a bolder vision, and declaring your readiness to play a bigger game. You're placing a big bet on yourself. Trying to accomplish all of this on your own makes it a far riskier leap. The relationships you invest in and the people you bring along with you are your safety net.

As you become more empowered, look for opportunities to empower others. Share career wins and war stories with women coming up alongside you and following behind—even if your experiences seem mundane to you. There's no way to predict when your words will be exactly what someone else needs to hear.

Be a role model, culture shifter, and bias buster too. Lead by example, use your voice to stand up for people who aren't being heard, and look for ways to help, guide, and support others in small ways every day. Give a copy of this book to your niece, mentee, daughter, employee, best friend, "best-kept secret" colleague, or mom. Drop a copy on your boss's desk.

Don't just kick open doors. Hold them open and invite others to step through.

Finally, if you want to leave a lasting leadership legacy, don't just aspire to be a leader, or even a leader who develops other leaders. Make an exponential impact by becoming an L^3: a leader who develops leaders who develop leaders.

> **Don't just kick open doors. Hold them open and invite others to step through.**

**BE A LEADER
WHO DEVELOPS LEADERS
WHO DEVELOP LEADERS**

Appendix

Reviewing the 12 Common Missteps
(and How to Avoid Them)

Throughout this book, I have explained 12 of the common career-limiting missteps I see made by even the most streetwise emerging leaders—and the strong Leaderly Moves to make instead. Here's a recap for you to use as a quick reference:

- **Misstep 1:** Waiting for permission or an invitation to be a leader
  Leaderly Move: Recognizing the leader in yourself (Chapter 1)

- **Misstep 2:** Doing work that will never make you shine
  Leaderly Move: Owning your leadership strengths (Chapter 2)

- **Misstep 3:** Being good at a lot of things and famous for none of them
  Leaderly Move: Claiming a niche that aligns your strengths and passions with your value to your organization (Chapter 3)

- **Misstep 4:** Allowing others to define your reputation
  Leaderly Move: Designing how you want to be perceived (Chapter 4)

- **Misstep 5:** Getting stuck with a dead-end brand
  Leaderly Move: Making your brand scalable (Chapter 4)

- **Misstep 6:** Acting like a doer, not a leader
  Leaderly Move: Shifting your mindset from "me" to "we" (Chapter 5)

- **Misstep 7:** Accepting low-visibility assignments
  Leaderly Move: Creating career-defining moments (Chapter 6)

- **Misstep 8:** Downplaying your accomplishments
  Leaderly Move: Amplifying the accomplishments that align with your aspirations (Chapter 7)

- **Misstep 9:** Working when you should be relationship building
  Leaderly Move: Building a supportive, influential network (Chapter 8)

- **Misstep 10:** Avoiding office politics
  Leaderly Move: Practicing positive political skills (Chapter 8)

- **Misstep 11:** Being overmentored and undersponsored
  Leaderly Move: Attracting the advocacy of influential sponsors (Chapter 9)

- **Misstep 12:** Climbing the ladder and then kicking it away
  Leaderly Move: Lifting others up as you rise (Chapter 9)

THERE'S MORE

Visit www.jomiller.com/womanofinfluence for a wealth of extra resources that I couldn't possibly cram into the book, including worksheets, checklists, stories, videos, and more.

Acknowledgments

Writing a book is a team activity—more so than I ever anticipated. I'm fortunate to be surrounded by kick-arse women. My editor Cheryl Segura championed the book at McGraw-Hill. Elizabeth Dougherty read every word of the manuscript—her meticulous feedback, publishing expertise, and killer insights were invaluable. Alicia Simons helped me turn a decade-old idea into a grown-up book proposal. Illustrator Marichiel Boudwin captured just the right amount of sass.

More than 150 leaders generously shared their stories and wisdom gained from kicking open doors—then holding them open and inviting others to step through.

At Be Leaderly, operations and marketing rock star Angie Klein always had (and has) my back. My research partner Selena Rezvani provided perspective-transforming "ahas" whenever I got stuck.

I extend my deepest gratitude to the hundreds of thousands of women in the Be Leaderly community who have attended my workshops, participated in a webinar, listened to a keynote, read drafts and given feedback, or passed along my newsletter—and especially those who asked, "Is there a book about this?" Let's keep lifting each other up.

I'm lucky to have Cat Cantrill, Sandy Stewart, Maria Camarotti, Olivia Shen Green, Cate Huston, Bushra Anjum, and my global Aussie Posse in my support squad. And, I am amazed and inspired by Melanie Dancer, Shannon Skoumbourdis, Naomi Hassam, Victoria Strike, and Lisa Woodhead, my force-of-nature sister.

Thanks to my mum, Kay Miller, I grew up surrounded by books and dreamed of writing my own. You're an unstoppable force of creativity and activism.

Thanks to my dad, John Miller, who shaped my career by saying, "If you can write well and speak well, people will think of you as an expert." You always believed I could accomplish anything I wanted to.

Most of all, I want to thank my husband, Chris Turkovich. The care and feeding of an author is a serious business, and you did it beautifully, with help from fur-baby Pepper. Love you both heaps.

Notes

INTRODUCTION

1. Claudio Fernández-Aráoz, Andrew Roscoe, and Kentaro Aramaki, "Turning Potential into Success: The Missing Link in Leadership Development," *Harvard Business Review*, November-December 2017, https://hbr.org/2017/11/turning-potential -into-success-the-missing-link-in-leadership-development.
2. Jo Miller, Be Leaderly, surveys of 250 senior women in tech in 2018 and 2019.
3. Ibid.
4. Jo Miller, Be Leaderly, surveys of 1,210 workshop attendees and 400 keynote attendees; and Jo Miller and Selena Rezvani, *Out of the Comfort Zone: How Women and Men Size up Stretch Assignments—and Why Leaders Should Care*, Be Leaderly, https://beleaderly.com/stretch-assignments/.

CHAPTER 1

1. Michael Bazigos and Jim Harter, "Revisiting the Matrix Organization," *McKinsey Quarterly*, January 2016, https://www.mckinsey.com/business-functions /organization/our-insights/revisiting-the-matrix-organization.
2. Claudio Fernández-Aráoz, Andrew Roscoe, and Kentaro Aramaki, "Turning Potential into Success: The Missing Link in Leadership Development," *Harvard Business Review*, November-December 2017, https://hbr.org/2017/11/turning -potential-into-success-the-missing-link-in-leadership-development.
3. Susan M. Jensen and Fred Luthans, "Entrepreneurs as Authentic Leaders: Impact on Employees' Attitudes," *Leadership & Organization Development Journal*, vol. 27, no. 8, December 2006, doi: 10.1108/01437730610709273.
4. Adapted from Claudio Feser, Fernanda Mayol, and Ramesh Srinivasan, "Decoding Leadership: What Really Matters," *McKinsey Quarterly*, January 2015, https:// www.mckinsey.com/featured-insights/leadership/decoding-leadership-what -really-matters.

CHAPTER 2

1. Michele Drayton, "On the Way Up the Corporate Ladder, Carry Your 'Pearls' Advises Morgan Stanley's Carla Harris," *Theglasshammer*, n.d., https://theglass hammer.com/2014/07/15/on-the-way-up-the-corporate-ladder-carry-your -pearls-advises-morgan-stanleys-carla-harris/, accessed April 28, 2019.

2. Marcus Buckingham and Donald O. Clifton, *Now, Discover Your Strengths* (New York: Free Press, 2001).

3. Peter Flade, Jim Asplund, and Gwen Elliot, "Employees Who Use Their Strengths Outperform Those Who Don't," *Gallup Workplace*, October 8, 2015, https://www.gallup.com/workplace/236561/employees-strengths-outperform-don.aspx.

4. Susan Sorenson, "How Employees' Strengths Make Your Company Stronger," *Gallup Business Journal*, February 20, 2014, https://news.gallup.com/businessjournal/167462/employees-strengths-company-stronger.aspx.

5. Marcus Buckingham, "How to Do What You Love," *Marcus Buckingham*, n.d., https://www.marcusbuckingham.com/rwtb/how-to-do-what-you-love/, accessed April 27, 2019.

6. Jo Miller, Be Leaderly, Surveys of 1,210 workshop attendees.

7. Flade, Asplund, and Elliot, "Employees Who Use Their Strengths."

8. Christopher Peterson et al., "Strengths of Character and Work." In the *Oxford Handbook of Positive Psychology and Work*, edited by P. A. Linley, Susan Harrington, and Nicola Garcea (Oxford: Oxford University Press, 2009), doi: 10.1093/oxfordhb/9780195335446.001.0001.

CHAPTER 3

1. Adapted from Lee W. Frederiksen, Elizabeth Harr, and Sylvia S. Montgomery, *The Visible Expert* (Reston, VA: Hinge Research Institute, 2014), https://hingemarketing.com/uploads/hinge-book-visibleexpert.pdf.

2. John Hagel et al., "If You Love Them, Set Them Free: Why Building the Workforce You Need for Tomorrow Means Giving Them Wings to Fly Today," *Deloitte Insights*, June 6, 2017, https://www2.deloitte.com/insights/us/en/topics/talent/future-workforce-engagement-in-the-workplace.html.

3. Paul A. O'Keefe, Carol S. Dweck, and Gregory M. Walton,"Implicit Theories of Interest: Finding Your Passion or Developing It?" *Psychological Science* (forthcoming), http://gregorywalton-stanford.weebly.com/uploads/4/9/4/4/49448111/okeefedweckwalton_2018.pdf.

4. Adapted from Jim Collins, *Good to Great: Why Some Companies Make the Leap and Others Don't* (New York: Harper Collins, 2001).

CHAPTER 4

1. *Urban Dictionary*, s.v. "bomb-ass," https://www.urbandictionary.com/define.php?term=Bomb%20ass, accessed April 27, 2019.

2. Alice Katwan, "4 Ways to Slow Down Your Career Clock and Still Get Ahead," *Working Mother*, September 19, 2016, https://www.workingmother.com/how-working-moms-can-slow-down-career-and-get-ahead.

3. Carla Harris, *The 2016 MAKERS Conference*, online video, MAKERS, https://www.makers.com/videos/56b113dce4b0717d92b26a6c, accessed April 27, 2019.

4. Matthew Hutson, "First Impressions Really Do Matter," *Boston Globe*, May 18, 2015, https://www.bostonglobe.com/ideas/2015/05/18/first-impressions-really-matter/elqLdg57Ftqw5n5jNxBH9N/story.html.

5. Jo Miller, Be Leaderly, in-session poll responses from 139 participants in 2018 branding workshops and webinars.

6. Hilary Burns, "4 'Pearls of Wisdom' on How to Succeed from a Wall Street Banker," *Business Journals*, November 11, 2014, https://www.bizjournals.com/bizjournals/how-to/growth-strategies/2014/11/carla-harris-morgan-stanley-pearls-of-wisdom.html.

7. Jo Miller, Be Leaderly, survey of 230 attendees at the 2018 Grace Hopper Celebration of Women in Computing Senior Women's Program.

8. LeanIn.org and McKinsey & Company, *Women in the Workplace 2018*, https://womenintheworkplace.com/, accessed April 28, 2019.

9. Lalah Delia, personal comment posted on Twitter.com, 10:24 a.m., October 29, 2018, https:// twitter.com/lalahdelia/status/1056959915221311488?lang=en.

10. Daniel P. Howrigan and Kevin B. MacDonald, "Humor as a Mental Fitness Indicator," *Evolutionary Psychology*, vol. 6, no. 4, 2008, pp. 652–666, https://journals.sagepub.com/doi/pdf/10.1177/147470490800600411.

11. Zak Stambor, "How Laughing Leads to Learning," *American Psychological Association*, vol. 37, no. 7, June 2006, p. 62, https://www.apa.org/monitor/jun06/learning.

12. Christopher Peterson et al., "Strengths of Character and Work." In the *Oxford Handbook of Positive Psychology and Work*, edited by P. A. Linley, Susan Harrington, and Nicola Garcea (Oxford: Oxford University Press, 2009), doi: 10.1093/oxfordhb/9780195335446.001.0001.

CHAPTER 5

1. John Gregory, "University of Louisville President Dr. Neeli Bendapudi," Kentucky Educational Television (KET), September 15, 2018, https://www.ket.org/public-affairs/university-louisville-president-dr-neeli-bendapudi/.

2. Claudio Fernández-Aráoz, Andrew Roscoe, and Kentaro Aramaki, "Turning Potential into Success: The Missing Link in Leadership Development," *Harvard Business Review*, November 2017, https://hbr.org/2017/11/turning-potential-into-success-the-missing-link-in-leadership-development.

3. Robert I. Mehr and Bob A. Hedges, *Risk Management in the Business Environment* (Homewood, IL: Irwin, 1963).

CHAPTER 6

1. Joan C. Williams and Marina Multhaup, "For Women and Minorities to Get Ahead, Managers Must Assign Work Fairly," *Harvard Business Review*, March 5, 2018, https://hbr.org/2018/03/for-women-and-minorities-to-get-ahead-managers-must-assign-work-fairly.

2. Margie Warrell, "Take a Risk: The Odds Are Better Than You Think," *Forbes*, June 18, 2013, https://www.forbes.com/sites/margiewarrell/2013/06/18/take-a-risk-the-odds-are-better-than-you-think/#2d1976d345c2.

3. Adapted from Jo Miller and Selena Rezvani, *Out of the Comfort Zone: How Women and Men Size up Stretch Assignments—and Why Leaders Should Care*, Be Leaderly, https://beleaderly.com/stretch-assignments/.

4. Catalyst, *Women in U.S. Corporate Leadership: 2003*, https://www.catalyst.org/wp-content/uploads/2019/01/Women_in_US_Corporate_Leadership.pdf, accessed April 28, 2019.

5. Claudio Fernández-Aráoz, "21st-Century Talent Spotting," *Harvard Business Review*, June 2014, https://hbr.org/2014/06/21st-century-talent-spotting.

6. Korn Ferry Institute, *Planning a Leadership Development Journey*, https://www.kornferry.com/institute/download/view/id/5103/aid/935, accessed April 28, 2019.

7. WorkSocial, *Women in the Workplace Study by McKinsey & Company*, November 11, 2017, https://www.worksocial.works/women-workplace-study-mckinsey-company/.

8. Catalyst, *Good Intentions, Imperfect Execution? Women Get Fewer of the "Hot Jobs" Needed to Advance*, Catalyst.org, November 21, 2012, https://www.catalyst.org/research/good-intentions-imperfect-execution-women-get-fewer-of-the-hot-jobs-needed-to-advance/.

9. Shelley Correll and Caroline Simard, "Research: Vague Feedback Is Holding Women Back," *Harvard Business Review*, April 29, 2016, https://hbr.org/2016/04/research-vague-feedback-is-holding-women-back.

10. LeanIn.org and McKinsey & Company, *Women in the Workplace 2016*, October 28, 2016, https://leanin.org/news-inspiration/wiw-2016.

11. J. K. Rowling, *Harry Potter and the Chamber of Secrets* (New York: Scholastic, 2000).

12. Adapted from Jo Miller, "4 Ways to Execute a Stretch Assignment Like a Rock Star," *Forbes*, December 16, 2017, https://www.forbes.com/sites/jomiller/2017/12/16/4-ways-to-execute-a-stretch-assignment-like-a-rock-star/.

CHAPTER 7

1. Shelley Correll and Lori Mackenzie, "To Succeed in Tech, Women Need More Visibility," *Harvard Business Review*, September 13, 2016, https://hbr.org/2016/09/to-succeed-in-tech-women-need-more-visibility.

2. Nancy M. Carter and Christine Silva, *Report: The Myth of the Ideal Worker: Does Doing All the Right Things Really Get Women Ahead?*, Catalyst.org, October 1, 2011, https://www.catalyst.org/research/the-myth-of-the-ideal-worker-does-doing-all-the-right-things-really-get-women-ahead/.

3. Carol Schmidt, "Bragging Rights: MSU Study Shows That Interventions Help Women's Reluctance to Discuss Accomplishments," (includes discussion of a study by Jessie L. Smith), Montana State University, January 10, 2014, https://www.montana.edu/news/12368/bragging-rights-msu-study-shows-that-interventions-help-women-s-reluctance-to-discuss-accomplishments.

4. Julie E. Phelan, Corrine A. Moss-Racusin, and Laurie A. Rudman, "Competent Yet out in the Cold: Shifting Criteria for Hiring Reflect Backlash Toward Agentic Women," *Psychology of Women Quarterly*, vol. 32, no. 4, December 2008, pp. 406–413, doi:10.1111/j.1471-6402.2008.00454.x; and Laurie Rudman and Peter Glick, "Prescriptive Gender Stereotypes and Backlash Toward Agentic Women, *Journal of Social Issues*, vol. 57, no. 4, December 17, 2002, pp. 743–762, doi:10.1111/0022-4537.00239.

5. Corinne A. Moss-Racusin and Laurie A. Rudman, "Disruptions in Women's Self-Promotion: The Backlash Avoidance Model," *Psychology of Women Quarterly*, vol. 34, no. 2, May 6, 2010, pp. 186–202, doi: 10.1111/j.1471-6402.2010.01561.x.

6. Jessi L. Smith and Meghan Huntoon, "Women's Bragging Rights: Overcoming Modesty Norms to Facilitate Women's Self-Promotion," *Psychology of Women Quarterly*, vol. 38, no. 4, December 20, 2013, pp. 447–459, doi:10.1177/0361684 313515840.

7. Lee W. Frederiksen, Elizabeth Harr, and Sylvia S. Montgomery, *The Visible Expert* (Reston, VA: Hinge Research Institute, 2014), https://hingemarketing.com/uploads /hinge-book-visibleexpert.pdf.

8. Vanessa Boris, "What Makes Storytelling So Effective for Learning?" Harvard Business Publishing, Corporate Learning, blog, December 20, 2017, https://www .harvardbusiness.org/what-makes-storytelling-so-effective-for-learning/.

9. "The Clever Strategy Obama's Women Staffers Came up with to Make Sure They Were Being Heard," Women in the World, September 14, 2016, https://womenin theworld.com/2016/09/14/the-clever-strategy-obamas-women-staffers-came -up-with-to-make-sure-they-were-being-heard/.

10. Marcial Losada and Emily Heaphy, "The Role of Positivity and Connectivity in the Performance of Business Teams: A Nonlinear Dynamics Model," *American Behavioral Scientist*, vol. 47, no. 6, February 1, 2004, pp. 740–765, doi: 10.1177 /0002764203260208.

CHAPTER 8

1. Amy Cuddy, "Your Body Language Shapes Who You Are," *HuffPost: The Blog*, January 10, 2013, https://www.huffpost.com/entry/body-language_b_2451277?ir =TED+Weekends&ref=topbar.

2. Joanna Barsh, Susie Cranston, and Rebecca A. Craske, "Centered Leadership: How Talented Women Thrive," *McKinsey Quarterly*, September 2008, https:// www.mckinsey.com/featured-insights/leadership/centered-leadership-how -talented-women-thrive.

3. Kenneth R. Rosen, "How to Recognize Burnout Before You're Burned Out," *New York Times*, September 5, 2017, https://www.nytimes.com/2017/09/05/smarter -living/workplace-burnout-symptoms.html?module=inline.

4. Yang Yang, Nitesh V. Chawla, and Brian Uzzi, "A Network's Gender Composition and Communication Pattern Predicts Women's Leadership Success," *Proceedings of the National Academy of Sciences* (PNAS), vol. 116, no. 6, February 5, 2019, pp. 2033–2038, https://www.pnas.org/content/116/6/2033.

5. Cuddy, "Your Body Language."

6. *Merriam-Webster*, s.v. "office politics," https://www.merriam-webster.com/dictionary/office%20politics.

7. "Women Reveal Their Biggest Roadblocks to Career Satisfaction and Success in New Survey Released by Citi and LinkedIn," *Business Wire*, May 30, 2013, https://www.businesswire.com/news/home/20130530005738/en/Women-Reveal-Biggest-Roadblocks-Career-Satisfaction-Success.

8. Marian N. Ruderman and Patricia J. Ohlott, *Standing at the Crossroads: Next Steps for High-Achieving Women* (San Francisco: Jossey-Bass, 2002).

9. Erin Burt, "Seven Career Killers," *Kiplinger*, updated January 2014, https://www.kiplinger.com/article/saving/T012-C006-S001-seven-career-killers.html.

10. Jean Brittain Leslie and William A. Gentry, *Women and Political Savvy: How to Build and Embrace Fundamental Leadership Skill*, White Paper, Center for Creative Leadership, https://www.ccl.org/wp-content/uploads/2016/10/Women PoliticalSavvy.pdf, accessed April 29, 2019.

11. *FSU News*, "Want to Get Ahead at Work? Hone Your Political Skills, Says FSU Professor," includes interview with Pamela Perrewé, Florida State University, https://www.fsu.edu/news/2006/04/26/political.skills/, accessed April 29, 2019.

12. Adapted from Michelle Schubnel and Michael Charest, Coach & Grow R.I.C.H. Client Attraction and Enrollment Program.

13. Minda Zetlin, "How to Network Like You Really Mean It." *Inc.*, March 24, 2014, https://www.inc.com/minda-zetlin/8-things-power-networkers-do-make-connections.html.

CHAPTER 9

1. Herminia Ibarra, Nancy M. Carter, and Christine Silva, "Why Men Still Get More Promotions Than Women," *Harvard Business Review*, September 2010, https://hbr.org/2010/09/why-men-still-get-more-promotions-than-women.

2. Jennifer Alsever, "Want to Move up in the Business World? Get a Sponsor," *Fortune*, May 21, 2012, http://fortune.com/2012/05/21/want-to-move-up-in-the-business-world-get-a-sponsor/.

3. Sylvia Ann Hewlett et al., *The Sponsor Effect: Breaking Through the Last Glass Ceiling*, Harvard Business Review Research Report, December 2010, http://30 percentclub.org/wp-content/uploads/2014/08/The-Sponsor-Effect.pdf.

4. Sylvia Ann Hewlett, Maggie Jackson, and Ellis Cose with Courtney Emerson, *Vaulting the Color Bar: How Sponsorship Levers Multicultural Professionals into Leadership*, Center for Talent Innovation (CTI),October 1, 2012, http://www.talent innovation.org/publication.cfm?publication=1350.

5. Hewlett et al., *The Sponsor Effect*.

6. Megan Leonhardt, "Here's Why You Should Always Ask for a Raise," CNBC, June 4, 2018, https://www.cnbc.com/2018/06/04/why-you-should-always-ask-for-a-raise-odds-are-youll-get-it.html.

7. Hewlett et al., *The Sponsor Effect*.

8. Jenna Goudreau, "Why You Need a Sponsor—Not a Mentor—to Fast-Track Your Career," *Business Insider*, September 9, 2013, https://www.businessinsider.com/you-need-a-sponsor-to-fast-track-your-career-2013-9.

9. Sallie Krawcheck, "The One Key Difference Between Massive Success and a Face Plant," Linked In, October 28, 2013, https://www.linkedin.com/pulse/20131028114308-174077701-the-one-key-difference-between-massive-success-and-a-face-plant/.

10. Goudreau, "Why You Need a Sponsor."

11. Melissa J. Anderson, "Building a Culture of Sponsorship," *Evolved Employer*, June 13, 2012, http://evolvedemployer.com/building-a-culture-of-sponsorship/.

CONCLUSION

1. Grace Lee Boggs, interview by Bill Moyers, *Bill Moyers Journal*, PBS, online video, June 5, 2007, http://www.pbs.org/moyers/journal/06152007/watch3.html.

Index

NTT Innovation Institute Inc., 114

O

Office housework, 110
Office politics, 163–166
Operator Collective, 142
Optimizers, 99
Organizational chart, 166–169
Organizational culture, 137–138
Organizational values, 53–55
Out of the Comfort Zone (Be Leaderly), 116
Outsource It exercises:
  amplifying accomplishments, 149
  baseline brand, 70
  brand statement, 87
  career-defining opportunities, 126
  leadership catnip, 10
  leadership types, 18
  mindset shifts, 107
  niche, 58
  organization value, 55
  for sponsors, 195, 200
  strengths, 27–28, 32, 34–36
Overdelivering, 127–128
Overstretching, 117–118
Own It exercises:
  amplifying accomplishments, 138, 149
  baseline brand, 71
  brand evolution, 79, 82–83
  building trust, 162
  career-defining opportunities, 120, 125–126, 128
  doing to delegating, 98

leadership catnip, 9–10
leadership type, 18
mentor questions, 179
mentors vs. sponsors, 186
mindset shifts, 107
network development, 180
networking plan, 170
niche, 57–58
  for office politics, 165–166
  optimizer to transformer, 101–102
  order taker to rule breaker, 105
  organization value, 55
  passion development, 53
  paying it forward, 202
  shadow organization map, 169
  for sponsors, 195, 200
  strengths, 27–28, 30–31, 33, 35
  stretch opportunities, 116, 118
  tactician to strategist, 94–95
Oxegen Consulting, 39, 47

P

Pace, Cindy, 6–7, 114
Passions:
  and amplifying accomplishments, 133–134
  and change, 100–101
  developing, 51–52
  and niche assessment, 46–47
Paying it forward, 201–202, 207
People leaders, 13, 14–15, 80
Perception gap, viii–ix, x–xi, 69
Perrewé, Pamela, 164
Personal brand(s), 65–87
  and amplifying accomplishments, 136–137

225

About the Author

 **Jo Miller** is a globally renowned leading authority on women's leadership. She began her career with raw, unpolished ambition and learned the hard way about office politics and the difficulties of being a woman in a male-dominated environment. This led her to find her calling: helping women around the world overcome these types of obstacles and advance into positions of leadership and influence.

Through coaching, her own research, and fierce compassion, she developed a pragmatic, yet powerful roadmap to help women move from where they are in their careers to where they aspire to be. She's written this book to share this step-by-step process with even more women and to help readers present themselves as the talented, emerging leaders they already are. Or as she often says: don't be the best-kept secret in your organization.

Jo is the CEO of Be Leaderly, a firm focused on leadership development, consulting, and research initiatives to elevate women's voices at work. To support emerging women leaders anywhere in the world, Jo created a popular webinar series that blends leadership skills training with access to live conversations with senior executive women. Started in 2009, the series is viewed by participants in 900 locations in 30 countries.

A sought-after speaker, Jo delivers more than 70 presentations each year to audiences of up to 1,200 women. Her audiences span the globe, including North America, Latin America, Europe, Asia Pacific, and the

Middle East. Her clients include Bank of America, BP, eBay, GM, MetLife, Microsoft, Princeton University, the USDA, Verizon, and hundreds of other commercial, government, nonprofit, and academic organizations.

Jo coauthored the award-winning research study *Out of the Comfort Zone: How Women and Men Size up Stretch Assignments—and Why Leaders Should Care.*

Jo grew up in Australia, and she has been celebrating life free from breast cancer since 2016. She believes that when life hands you lemons, you should stuff them in your bra and sing "Ta-dah!"